# The Journey Less Traveled:

## *Choose To Turn Your Tragedy Into Triumph*

By

Loretta L. Harris

an imprint of
Children's Heart
Orlando, FL

Published By:

Children's Heart Publishing
Post Office Box 691223
Orlando, FL  32869-1223

Copyright © 2008 Loretta L. Harris

Editor: Ghostwriter Extraordinaire, LLC (www.GWExtra.com)

Proofreader: Michelle Harris, Orlando, FL

Book Cover Design: Marshall White, 3RT Productions

The Journey Less Traveled:
*Choose To Turn Your Tragedy Into Triumph*
ISBN 10: 0-9786681-5-4
ISBN 13: 978-0-9786681-5-0
Library of Congress Control Number: 2008906169

Published and printed in the United States of America

# DEDICATION

This book is dedicated to readers of all ages, cultures, and experiences. No matter what phase in this journey through life you find yourself, just know that you are predestined to overcome your adversity.

FSU Bookstore

8AM to 5PM

# — ACKNOWLEDGEMENTS —

I did not ask for this, but somehow I proved to be the best candidate for this journey. It would be impossible to travel this road without the love and support of my family and trusted friends. To my mother, my mentor and best friend for the past twenty-eight years - not to mention the three months dedicated exclusively to my recovery: words cannot express my love and admiration for you.

To my father, I have always admired the gifts that God has given you. May the Lord bless the ministry that He has called you to perform. To my sister, Michelle: without second thought, you placed your life, dreams, and goals on hold to relocate to Orlando and commit to my full recovery. I love you with all of my heart.

My baby sister and LPN during my most crucial hours, Cassandra: thank you for having my back and blessing me with a beautiful godson, Christian.

It's amazing how the human brain, during its semi-conscious state, selects events to commit to memory. To my oldest brother, Meshach, who secured the premises during the cold and long nights in the Intensive Care Unit: I remember the feeling of comfort I got from just knowing that you were present. Thank you for staying attentive to my every need.

To my baby brother, Kevin: thank you for rushing to my side and keeping hope alive in your heart.

Our time on earth is precious, and we are blessed to cross paths with those who can help us fan the flames of life. To my sisters, Tekoa and Sherrina: the news of your unselfish support and prayers sends chills up my spine to this day.

To the countless friends and colleagues who

refused to stop praying until they witnessed God bring me through: thank God for you.

To my Bishop, Edward Harris, my cousin Shea, and the dedicated church family of the First Apostolic Assembly of Pahokee: thank you for standing in the gap and rushing to my side.

To my local Pastors, Marvin and Deborah Jackson, and the phenomenal church family at the River of Life Christian Center: thank you for shaking the gates of hell on my behalf! You stepped in and never ceased to pray until the doctors changed their reports.

I appreciate the strength of my spiritual mentors, Pastors Marvin and Deborah Jackson, Mother Mary Neal, and Ms. Mina Ford, who heard the voice of the Lord say, "She shall live and not die." Thank you for speaking into my spirit those words of encouragement.

I also acknowledge the countless supporters who traveled to the hospital to encourage my family members during my darkest hours.

I encourage the readers of this book to open your hearts and minds as you read this genuine account of my struggle to turn what appeared to be tragedy into immeasurable triumph. No matter what phase in this journey through life you find yourself, just know that you are predestined to conquer the storms of life.

# FOREWORD

My profession requires that I deal with suffering on many levels, but nothing could have prepared me for the summer of 2006, when one of my most faithful congregants and students in the ministry was involved in an automobile accident. The next three months would be both impacting and life changing, as I personally witnessed Loretta go from near death to nothing short of a miraculous, but painful, recovery.

The readers of, **The Journey Less Traveled: Choose To Turn Your Tragedy Into Triumph** will gain tremendous insight from this literary masterpiece. Loretta's first-hand experience with trials and tribulations will answer many of the "whys" in life. Personal tragedy is difficult to grapple, especially when it seems like you are doing all God requires; nevertheless, how do you handle it when it seems God is unfair and cruel? Loretta's book answers one of the main riddles of life, "Why do good people suffer?" and much more. This is a must read for those who are dealing with the vicissitudes of life.

To witness Loretta's insight and strength throughout this ordeal has been amazing. **The Journey Less Traveled** will take you on your own journey of faith and self-discovery.

Marvin A. Jackson, B.A., B.S., M.Th.
Senior Pastor, River of Life CC

# TABLE OF CONTENTS

# INTRODUCTION

This journey through life is filled with great opportunities and many obstacles. The title of this book emerged during my quest to understand the reasons for the human struggle: why do bad things happen to good people? How do some people survive the hardship, and others do not? If there is a God, how can He sit back and allow such devastation? After two years, I still do not have the answers to these questions and countless others. After studying the lives of individuals such as Jesus Christ, Job, Dr. Martin Luther King, Rosa Parks, Oprah Winfrey, and President John F. Kennedy, I observed a common thread: perseverance.

It is so easy to call it quits when the odds are against you, but the determined person decides to take the journey less traveled. This decision refers to the conscious effort of the individual to push past the tragedy. Your tragedy may not be similar to my personal encounters, shared within the pages of this book; however, we all share a common experience: pain. Whether it is the pain of losing a loved one, the effects of a divorce, the betrayal of a trusted friend, bankruptcy, or a terminal illness, the decision to go forward can be difficult.

Throughout this journey, you will encounter - if you have not already - your day of adversity. As difficult as it may seem, you can turn your tragedy into triumph. I know that this statement may sound a bit clichéd, but trust me on this one. Triumph refers to the joy that one has over a victory. To walk in victory means that you have overcome your obstacle. Take, for example, a single mother on welfare with no money to feed her children. She may not have a job, but her children are able to eat every night. Are the situations surrounding this young mother fair? No, but her life is golden compared to the millions of other homeless and starving families. Count your blessings because, when you think you have it bad, someone else has it worse.

The greatest obstacle to your recovery is you! It is imperative that you change your perspective regarding your situation and develop a conqueror's mentality. To conquer means *to get possession of or seize control of by mental, physical, or moral force.* Never back down from adversity; the only step back allowed is the one taken to view your hardship from a different standpoint.

After surviving my car accident, I realized my moral obligation to reach out to the hurt and dying with a genuine account of my struggle to push past the tragedy. It was not easy; in fact, the decision had proven to be the most difficult task I had ever faced - and pray I will ever face - in this lifetime. In the end, it was all worth the fight. In the words of the renowned songwriter Marvin Sapp, "I'm wiser, stronger, and a better" person because of God's grace and my decision to take the road filled with travesty to make it to my destiny.

# CHAPTER ONE

## The Day Of The Accident

The choices that you make in life will definitely affect the outcome of your life and the lives of your loved ones. May 24, 2006, was teacher post-planning and a day I recognized two of my favorite students for their academic achievements. That morning, I awakened to the soft worship music playing on my disc player and conducted the usual routine of prayer at my prayer table before leaving for work. As I proceeded out the front door and turned around to secure the lock, I had no idea that I was never going to see my one bedroom apartment again. On that day, my mom decided not to go to work. That was not her usual protocol, but she followed her instincts and remained home. It was about 3:00 pm that evening when she received a phone call from Robert in the emergency room of Orlando Regional Medical Center with the news of her daughter's recent car accident. Unwilling to give further details, he insisted that she provide him with information regarding her closest relative. After pleading with Robert for more information, my mother gave him the number of my youngest sister, Cassandra.

As my mother struggled to dial Cassandra's telephone number, she could not imagine the degree of my injuries. Just to make it through the three-hour drive from Pahokee to Orlando with my older sister, Michelle, behind the wheel, my mother convinced herself that the injuries sustained could not be that serious. On that day, Cassandra had plans to go out with a friend, but they were undecided whether to have a nice dinner or see a movie. She felt an over-whelming need to go back to her house. Not knowing what to expect, she convinced her friend to return with her. Before she could get both feet in the door, the phone rang, but this ring felt different. When she picked up the phone, it was mom on the other end. Her voice sounded worried, and she strained to recite these very words: "Faith was in a serious car accident. Someone from the ER by the name of 'Mr. Robert' just called me and told me that she is located at Orlando Regional Medical Center."

One can only imagine the degree of confusion associated with the word, "serious." Cassandra struggled to keep her composure and immediately called the hospital. Unwilling to release the condition of her sister over the telephone, Cassandra learned that I was in a critical state. Weeping bitterly from this news, Cassandra had an empty feeling inside. Her friend was listening the entire time and perceived that she did not receive good news. After sharing the news about my condition, they rushed to the hospital. Crying uncontrollably, and with her heart racing, many thoughts were going through her mind, mainly: "Why did this have to happen to my sister?!"

In the meantime, my brother, Meshach, who we refer to as "Junior," was engaged in his routine workout at his local gym. He received a phone call

4

while on his way out of the facility. It was Cassandra on the other end. In a state of hysteria, she tried to inform Meshach of my critical condition: "Junior, Junior, Faith just got into a serious car accident!" Trying to grasp the meaning of this unexpected phone call, my brother repeatedly inquired about the seriousness of my condition. Junior recalled my previous car accident and wanted to believe in his heart that this, too, was not that bad. "Was it bad?" He asked. "Yes, they had to take her by a helicopter," my sister insisted. Without further delay, my brother jumped into his car and journeyed to the hospital. To bypass the traffic rush, Junior placed one of those flashing security lights (from his job as a security officer) on top of his car and sped down the highway. Thank God, no one stopped him.

My younger brother, Kevin, also resided in Palm Beach County at the time, over 200 miles away. Besides the back pain that he sustained the day before from a football injury, which restricted him to bed rest, he shared the same uncomfortable feelings as other family members. It was after three o'clock in the evening when Kevin received a phone call. It was our mom on the other end; odd that mom would call during her regular work hours. Kevin answered the phone in his usual joking mood. From the sound of her voice, he knew that something was terribly wrong. Kevin's giddy mood came to a screeching halt when he realized mom had been crying and apparently could not even begin her sentence. "What's wrong mom?" he asked, but nothing could prepare him for the news that he would hear. After hearing that I was involved in a serious car accident, Kevin immediately began preparing to travel to Orlando.

My devout friend and sister, Tekoa, returned home from work, took a seat on her sofa, and turned on the local news broadcast. Within seconds, a special news report aired. The news reporter stated that a tragic car accident had recently taken place. The reporter went on to state that someone was dead upon contact and that others had been taken to the hospital. Tekoa's body immediately chilled from this heart-wrenching news. She watched on as the news broadcast flashed a picture of the car involved in the accident. She saw a green Honda Civic literally crushed along a thin fence on the side of the highway. She immediately grabbed her keys and informed Chrystol, our mutual friend, that they had to get to the hospital, and for some reason she knew that, I was the victim. My friends cried and prayed as they took the journey towards the hospital. While en route, Chrystol received a call from one of the teachers who worked with us, and he confirmed what they were feeling: That was my green Honda, and I was the victim left in critical condition, fighting for my life. Airlifted by the Critical Care Transport, I experienced intermittent loss of consciousness on the way to the hospital.

That Thursday afternoon around three o'clock, I met adversity head-on, and death requested my life. The faith of my closest relatives and dearest friends held the belief that my work here on earth was not complete; therefore, God was not ready for me. My friends increased their prayers and petitioned God for my life. They finally arrived at the hospital, but the staff was not letting anyone through; actually, the doctors did not even know my name and had given me an alias. After Tekoa spoke with the nurse and told them that she was my sister, they were cleared to go back. Escorted into a special waiting room, my friends awaited the doctor's update. By that time, my estimated blood loss was 100 cc. In shock from the multiple fractures and multiple areas of bleeding, my body lay unstable in the operating room, Suite 3303 of the Burn Trauma Unit. There I was, at the mercy of

6

the almighty God. The Trauma Surgery Team was in the process of managing my care. Multiple services were conducting aggressive resuscitation and attempting to slow down the bleeding while keeping my airways open.

A church member contacted my pastors around four o'clock that afternoon to tell them about my car accident. The news really hit home for Pastor Deborah, whose own son had survived a life-threatening car accident over ten years ago. Disturbed to hear that I was in a critical state, she scurried to her bedroom closet to find something, anything to wear. After informing her husband, both were on their way to the hospital. While en route, Pastor Marvin made contact with Minister Wallace, the leader of the prayer ministry, and requested the formation of an immediate prayer chain. His direct instructions, "Rebuke the spirit of death because she shall live and not die." Upon their arrival at the hospital, my pastors greeted my friends. Their secondary concern was that my family members were aware of my condition. My pastors contacted their daughters, who were at the church, and requested that the entire youth department begin to pray. The young adults then offered a sincere prayer of recovery for their Sunday School teacher.

When Cassandra arrived, she was surprised to find the room filled with my friends, pastors, and co-workers. They told her that the four o'clock news aired footage of the car accident earlier that afternoon, including detailed information about the hit and run crash. The Chaplain entered the room and announced, "She may not make it." He asked for the family, and Cassandra said, "I am her sister." He looked at her and said, "Your sister is in a very critical stage; she is bleeding internally, and the doctors cannot stop the bleeding. They transfused four pints of blood, and she is still losing blood fast! She may not make it; at this point, what we need to do is pray." He began to name countless organs damaged or lacerated in my body and numerous bones either crushed or broken. At this point, Cassandra felt faint; she thought that she was going to die. Her mind reminisced on all the times that her body was sick, and how her sister had laid hands on her and prayed for her healing. She thought about all the advice shared throughout her twenty-four years. Cassandra could not remember a time that her sister needed her, until this very moment. Along with a prayer in her heart, Cassandra promised the Lord that if He brought her sister through this she would be a better person.

My godmother, Mary Neal, learned about my car accident from her son one or two hours after it occurred. The headline of the car crash was the highlight of the evening news, and once she witnessed the news flash she did not know how to react. The feeling that came over her was indescribable, and she wanted both to scream and faint. Her daughter-in-law rushed to her side for moral support. While preparing to travel to the hospital, my godmother cried and prayed in her heart. As she was praying and pleading to God, she heard in her spirit, "She shall live and not die." That was all the confirmation that she needed. Immediately, she dried her eyes and traveled to the hospital. When Mother Neal arrived at the hospital about six o'clock that evening, everyone was in the waiting room of the Burn Trauma unit. At that time, I was in surgery and in a very critical state. Mother Neal sat in her quiet corner, praying and trying to hold back the tears. She dared to believe the words that she heard before she left home, "She shall live and not die."

Shortly after 6:30 that evening, with just the clothes on their backs and the bare necessities, my mother and sister opened the door of the emergency room, only to witness Cassandra, Meshach, my godmother, and the lineup of close friends, church members, and co-workers already awaiting the doctor's update. In the meantime, the orthopedic surgeons were in the operating room doing as much as possible to control my unstable bones. They began by closing the 15 cm wound on my upper left arm. They then placed an external fixator on my left leg to allow proper alignment of my fractured bones. The trauma that my body endured was immense, and I developed abdominal compartment syndrome, a clinical disease that results from elevated intra-abdominal pressure due to free fluid collecting at the abdominal cavity (Medical, W. T., n.d.). If untreated, the results can be multi-system organ failure and patient death. Immediate surgery was the only option. Doctors proceeded to make a vertical incision in the center of my stomach, starting below my breast and ending at my bikini line. My stomach remained open for a several days, allowing my swollen organs room to breathe.

Hours passed before the doctor came forward to produce a medical update. After a brief introduction, the doctor proceeded to review the list of injuries to my body. I suffered a complex laceration of the liver, extra peritoneal bladder rupture, multiple pelvic fractures, left tibia-fibula fracture with the bones protruding through the skin in several places, along with a crushed anklebone. Not allowing much time for questions, he continued with his graphic account: I sustained a mild brain injury, fracture to the left forearm, upper arm lacerations, multiple lacerations to the left face and lower extremities, right tibial wound down to the bone, and left knee trauma. The doctor warned my family that it was possible I would not be able to see out my left eye again.

Finally, he hit my family with the most disheartening news: they were not expecting me to make it through the night. The doctor's last words encouraged the family to start praying because it was going to take a miracle. Once those words left the doctor's mouth, my family - unable to imagine life without their Faith and with their spirits heavy and hearts burdened - went into immediate intercession; death was not an option. International prayer chains formed rapidly, with contacts throughout the state of Florida, other states with family members and friends, and beyond the Caribbean islands. The intercessory prayer team at the River of Life initiated a 24-hour prayer watch in the waiting room of the hospital. Despite the many complaints from the facility regarding the noise levels, everyone was praying around the clock. There was only one goal: "She shall live and not die!"

Finally, around ten o'clock that night, doctors requested that the mother of the injured party come forward to identify the victim. When called to view the damaged body of her second child, my mother requested the presence and support of my local church pastor, Marvin Jackson. He agreed, and they entered that cold Burn Trauma unit together. Horrified by what she witnessed, my mother felt as though the life were sucked out of her body. It was as if she encountered an out-of-body experience. She knew that she was walking, but she felt no legs holding her up. My body was swollen three times its normal size, and I was beyond recognition. Only my face remained uncovered, while the rest of my body lay wrapped up in the hospital sheets, marred and broken. My hair was scattered and matted with blood. Pieces of glass remained glued to my face, held in place by the dried blood. Trying to make sense of the whole ordeal, Pastor Jackson walked up to my bed and whispered in my ear, "You can't die because you are not done yet."

Distraught by the apparent destruction of her

daughter's body, my mom announced, "Lord, she didn't make it anywhere yet." There were cords and machines everywhere, and the entire ceiling was covered with machinery. My lips were swollen and sealed tight, and mother wanted to know if I still had my pearly whites, but the doctors were not equipped to answer that question and many others. No one prepared for this day of adversity, especially my mother. Weakened and disarrayed, my mother turned to my pastor and requested a word of prayer. She walked out of that hospital room with the vivid image of her daughter's unrecognizable body. The audience awaited the update, but they could only console my mother as she tried to convey what she had witnessed. Around ten o'clock that night, the doctors allowed my mother to escort individual family members to my room for a short visit. Forced to be strong, onlookers could not fathom the depth of the pain my mother carried in her heart. Mourning vibrated throughout the entire Burn Trauma unit at the sight of my condition. The degree of sorrow was comfortless; no one slept, and everyone prayed.

Before midnight, Cassandra gathered enough strength to pick up the phone and inform our family in Pahokee, Florida, of the tragic event. Disturbed by the late-night call, our grandfather, Bishop Edward Harris, answered the phone, "San, what's wrong? You've never called our house this time at night." After hearing the news that his granddaughter had been in a serious car accident, my grandfather extended his hands to heaven and offered a sincere cry to the Lord, "Jesus, Jesus, Jesus, Faity!" There were no other words suitable for this level of emergency, so he continued to call on the name of the Lord. His cries awakened my grandmother, who joined him in petitioning the Lord for my healing. After countless hours of intercession, my grandfather was comforted by a sweet presence of peace, which allowed him to know that I would indeed be all right. In the time of trouble, the Lord promises in His word that He will give strength to His people and bless His people with peace (Psalms 30:5, KJV). My grandfather kept this reassurance in his heart and never doubted God's ability to restore his granddaughter.

# CHAPTER TWO

## Why Am I Here?

### Living a Nightmare

The first twenty-four hours of a trauma patient are critical. During these critical hours, doctors can determine if the patient has a fighting chance at life. I faced a high risk of mortality with each surgery. Each time that I appeared to get better, my recovery was short-lived as I took a turn for the worse. My family struggled to keep their faith in God, but doctors constantly reminded them to expect the worst. If I were to survive this degree of trauma, doctors insisted that I would require medical treatment for the rest of my life. The best that Central Florida had to offer worked devotedly to restore my broken body. I suffered from acute respiratory failure and required a ventilator. On May 25, doctors inserted a bilateral pigtail chest tube to assist my collapsed lungs. That same day, doctors placed filters in both legs to prevent blood clots. The next day, doctors inserted a naso-enteric feeding tube. My mother and sister, Michelle, gave the doctors their full cooperation regarding each medical procedure. Doctors informed my family of the risks, benefits, and alternatives to each surgery before allowing them to sign the consent forms.

My car accident qualified as a high profile case. The media were constantly contacting the hospital, posing as family members or close friends just to get an update on my condition. Individuals went to the extremes and pretended to be my significant other in order to gain access to my room. The guest list dwindled down to a select few for my protection. Unannounced guests, along with spectators, were quickly sent away with no further explanation. My family became the gatekeepers of my soul, and they risked no negative words spoken in my presence. The surgeries continued, and on May 27, with the cleansing and closure of my left knee, right leg wound, and ulnar fractures in the left forearm, a metal plate was inserted in my left arm and leg. On May 28, my plastic surgeon worked countless hours in an effort to repair my facial lacerations. He applied sutures to my forehead, face, and left ear. And on June 1, well over a full week, doctors finally closed my open abdomen.

Surgeons repaired my pelvic wing on June 2 and inserted a seven-hole pelvic recon plate. On June 9, my orthopedic surgeons conducted work on my tibia-fibula fractures and removed the external fixator. Updates of my condition were given on a regular basis to those dedicated to prayer. Once the news went out that I was recovering well, I slipped into a worse state. On one occasion, I began to bleed from the mouth and nose. The next day, doctors conducted an exploratory laparotomy, involving a surgical incision through the abdominal wall. This medical procedure revealed a serious case of erosive gastric bleeding. Doctors were unable to determine the actual source of bleeding, and for a brief moment, the problem ceased. Unfortunately, I continued to throw up blood, and on June 15, I received two units of packed red blood cells for acute blood loss anemia.

It was the midnight calls that were the most dreadful; family members and friends did not know what to expect. By June 16, after countless efforts to stop the internal bleeding, doctors decided to conduct a partial gastrectomy, which involved approximately 80% stomach removal. This was the most life-threatening surgery I had to undergo. I faintly recall the doctors discussing this procedure with me. After three weeks, I had not gained full mental awareness of my condition. Doctors awaited the arrival of my mother and sister, Michelle, to provide this medical update and receive their consent. Doctors reminded my family of the increased mortality rate. Once approved, I had to drink a huge cup of liquid to pinpoint the exact areas of bleeding. Once again, my body was carried to the operating room for surgery, and my intercessors were made aware during the early morning hours of my condition and upcoming surgery. Doctors were amazed at my constant comeback and reported my stable condition. My body totally submitted to the process and offered no resistance, which resulted in no further complications. Orlando Regional Medical Center provided records revealing over one dozen surgeries performed on my body.

## Shattered Pieces

I was in a semiconscious state throughout the course of the first three weeks. I had no memory of where I was or how I got there. I suffered from a constant fever, bacterial pneumonia, severe diarrhea, and high blood pressure. Doctors and nurses were constantly in and out of my room, conducting routine checkups while administering numerous medications such as lopressors for high blood pressure, dulcolax suppositories to maintain my digestive system, tobramycin to treat the pneumonia, and lovenox morphine sulfate to subdue the pain. I scanned the room in an attempt to gain my awareness. I faintly recall recognizing my immobilized body connected to an enormous electronic machine, which had countless cords dispatched to every area on my body. My ears became immune to the constant "beeping" sound of the machines. I had a breathing device inserted into my throat to aid my breathing, along with an intravenous tube in my arm. There was a feeding tube placed through my nostril and a tube at the top of my head to allow drainage. I was disillusioned by my present condition and in constant need of medication to relieve me of my pain.

Thoughts scattered through my brain, "What am I doing here?" and "What is going on?" With every passing moment, I tried to recall the events leading up to my hospitalization, but it was to no avail. My family faced the difficult task of refreshing my memory. "You were in a car accident on your way from work," whispered Michelle. I listened, but nothing made sense. "What happened to my car?" I asked. "It was totaled," she said. I knew that there was more to this story; I was just too tired to ask. Each day I struggled to remember something, anything that would help me understand my reason for being in this critical condition. It was apparent that I sustained severe injuries from this wreck because I did not have the strength to lift my limbs. It was then that I realized the weight of the cast on both my left arm and leg. The pink suture bands and staples that held my stomach together irritated me greatly. Oblivious to my condition, I ripped the naso-enteric feeding tube from my stomach and through my nostril. I paid dearly for this daring act and had to endure three days of bed restraint, which involved the banning of my hands and absolutely no food until my stomach healed. I whined and cried from an empty stomach, which was very difficult for my family to witness. I craved every dinner plate that passed my room. My sister begged the doctors to reinsert my feeding tube, but they were not giving in. Doctors feared that as I gained awareness of my condition I would do more harm than good. My behavior I cannot rationalize, but one thing was clear: my body took a beating, but my spirit went untouched. I realized that the hospital was not my home.

"Why am I here? I should be somewhere teaching my students." That was it! My first connection to the real world was the memories of my students. I remembered working on a class project. My thoughts scrambled around to my jump drive. "Michelle where is my jump drive? I promised my students that I would publish their books." My sister looked at me only to repeat the same information, "Everything was destroyed with the car." This answer yielded my usual response, "Awe, man!" Although this would not be our last time visiting this discussion, this was the first time that the impact of this accident really hit home. Mentally, I knew that something was wrong because I heard myself repeating the same questions. Later on, I learned that I sustained a mild brain injury, which resulted in temporary short-term memory loss. The tube on the top left side of my head confirmed this injury.

Since my last memories were of my students' project, I tried my best to build on that piece of information. My sister said that I was returning from work at the time of the accident, but the question is where was I going? Home or back to work? This vital piece of information would make a huge difference in my complete reaction to this tragedy. Then it hit me like a lightning bolt: the last thing that I remembered was spending time with my students and colleagues at lunch. I was convinced that the accident had to be after lunch. I felt confident about this piece of information that I struggled to collect.

I tried vigorously to restore my memory with key events leading up to my accident. I bombarded what was left of my memory with questions such as, "What route did I take home?" and "Is everyone else safe?" and "Whose fault was the accident?" In between my routine checkups, these questions and so many more disturbed my innermost being. I repeatedly dismissed all doubts. I was sure that my family would inform me if other parties were involved. I was certain that there was no need to probe anyone for further explanations. To be quite honest, I was too afraid to hear their response.

## Pain Zone

I did not have all the answers, but I knew the solution to this pain problem. There was such an intense degree of pain gravitating through my body. To this day, I cannot explain where the pain originated. It was as if my entire body doused itself into a river called Pain. I was grateful for the few occasions when the nurse rushed into the room with my scheduled dose of morphine. Those were my better days. Most times, my body entered into what I refer to as the "Pain Zone." On those days, I had to lay in wait, forced to absorb the pain. Unable to speak, I made grunts and used body gestures to signal my discomfort. During their overnight shifts, my family members became my voice and alerted the assigned nurse to my condition.

There I was, in that dark and freezing room, lying on that hard hospital bed with those thin sheets. I slept a lot and oftentimes drifted off in the middle of a visit. I felt minimal pain when I slept. The times when I woke up, I awakened to pain in its highest degree. Once I learned my tolerance level for pain, I requested early injections and prayed that the nurses obliged. I guess they really had no choice after the persistent interruptions of the buzzer. Once relieved of this torture, I would mentally drift off into the abyss and awaken the next morning to relive the frustrations all over again.

## The Nurse From Hell

My soul was in such confusion, and, after about three weeks, I still did not gain full understanding about my condition. My family members were taking shifts throughout the day to ensure that I received twenty-four hours of adequate care. On one occasion, a nurse I refer to as, "the nurse from hell" left me unattended. My family walked into my room at the exact moment that the breathing device malfunctioned, and I was left stifling for air. They alerted the hospital and rushed to my aid in an attempt to adjust the machine. When confronted about her negligence, the nurse denied her awareness of my condition and failure to hear the alarm.

This nurse gave much resistance, insisting that I was okay and that there was no need for immediate attention. I have two sisters, one of which is in the nursing field. My baby sister, Cassandra, a licensed practical nurse who was pregnant at the time, handled this particular situation. She insisted on the nurse's immediate reassignment because of her negligence. After going through the appropriate personnel, the hospital granted the request of my family members.

## My Favorite Nurse

I will never forget one particular nurse. Her name is Jen. Nurse Jen was a middle-aged African American woman who wore nice long braids and spoke with an English accent. She rushed to my aid every time I called. She was there to dry my eyes when I cried from the cleansing of my stomach wounds and assured me that everything was going to be all right. One day, Nurse Jen came into my room and announced that she had to administer a rectal suppository. I lacked bowel movement for a couple days, and the thought of having a suppository scared me.

My mind flashed back to the days when I had to sit in my own feces because I could not get a nurse to the room quick enough to supply my bedpan. Doctors feared that I suffered from gastroenteritis, an acute diarrhea that, if untreated, has the potential to cause death. I was relieved to learn that my case was not that severe. After going through this level of humiliation, I absolutely refused to repeat the cycle. With tears in my eyes, I pled with the nurse's assistant, Sandy, in an attempt to avoid the suppository. I shared my experiences with diarrhea, and within a few minutes, we were both sobbing like babies. The door swung open, and Nurse Jen entered with a surprised look on her face. I told her my reasons for not wanting the suppository, and we finally reached a consensus. I had one day to produce a bowel movement. If I did not experience a bowel movement within twenty-four hours, Nurse Jen would administer the rectal suppository.

I released a sigh of relief, convinced that this bowel movement was my only hope. Over the previous month, I had felt like I lost complete control over my body, but that night I spoke to my body and declared that it was time to cooperate with this process. All I needed was a slight movement of my bowels. I was willing to take anything, even the slightest stain on the bed sheets. The next day, I must have requested the bedpan over three times. Later on that evening, after several false alarms, my bowels finally decided to move. It was like the Fourth of July, and I wanted to celebrate. That bowel movement served a greater purpose; it was an indication that I was regaining the normal functions of my body.

## Time to Speak

Eventually, my blood pressure decreased, and doctors weaned me off the ventilator. I retained my tracheotomy tube, and my doctor ordered that I receive periodic breathing treatments. Another opportunity presented itself, and, once again, Nurse Jen came to my rescue. My mom and I laugh about this particular incident, which was the beginning of my gaining some form of independence, but also the return of "Bossy Faith." Early in the afternoon, a young woman whose name I do not remember entered my room with a small purple box in her hand. She told me that my doctors ordered a gadget that would allow me to speak. I was ecstatic after hearing the news. She removed the device from the box and walked over to my bed. After she inserted the device into my tracheotomy tube, she insisted that I speak. Well, I started by saying, "Hello." I could not believe the echo that I heard. It was my voice! I glanced at my mother, who was smiling from ear to ear.

Left alone to bond with my new toy, my family and I seized the opportunity to engage in meaningful conversations. For a brief moment, we all forgot about the tragedy that interrupted our individual lives, and we focused on the present joy of hearing me speak again. Shortly afterward, the young woman returned and interrupted the festivities. She insisted that I take out the device and return it to the purple box. Well, I was not having it. After six speechless weeks filled with agony, frustration, and pain, I felt that it was my time to speak. I immediately burst into tears and demanded that I keep the device next to my bed. After her reluctance, I requested the second opinion of my nurse.

Once Nurse Jen entered my room, I explained the situation. What a great nurse. She walked over to my bed, gave me the purple box, and said that it was my voice and that I could speak anytime I wanted. The purple box was officially in my possession. This voiceless patient felt empowered. Although this did not solve all of my problems, I was relieved to know that I would be able to voice my concerns and communicate with my family.

# CHAPTER THREE

## Tragedy Has No Face

### Denial Phase

*Denial functions as a buffer after unexpected shocking news, allows patient to collect himself, and, with time, mobilize other, less radical defenses. (Kubler-Ross, 1969)*

**D**uring that six-week period in the step down unit of Orlando Regional Medical Center, I clearly remember bargaining with my sister, Michelle, to remove the bed rails. I explained my rationale for the request: I wanted to walk around my hospital room and pray, something that I practiced in the privacy of my home. I did not realize it then, but deep down inside I wanted to get back to the communication and fellowship I shared with God. My sister constantly reminded me of my inability to walk without my doctor's consent. After several failed attempts, I insisted on just swinging my legs over the bed for a few minutes. I was in complete denial. The cast on my left leg and bandages on my right leg did not convince me of my limited mobility. I was suffering from an acute denial disorder, and my mind refused to accept my present condition.

Several weeks had passed since my car accident, and I found it very difficult to accept all of the injuries that my body sustained. This denial soon evolved into a truth or dare challenge. The removal of my feeding tube was not enough. I soon attempted the removal of the breathing device. The first instance shocked my mother, who gave me a very stern and direct warning. After my hand encompassed the tube, she insisted that, once removed, that would be the end of my life. Still under heavy medication, I gripped the tube yet again, and this time, with tears in her eyes, mom begged me to unhand the tube and not to touch it. Clearly, I was not in my "right state of mind." I knew that tears symbolized hurt, and someone who I loved was experiencing hurt from my actions. I did not want to hurt her, so I released the tube.

## Fear of Isolation

*We are pressed on every side by troubles, but we are not crushed. We are perplexed, but not driven to despair. (2 Corinthians 4:8, NLT)*

The trials of life will leave you desolate. Your altered condition will require immediate assistance, but at times, you just want to be alone. This is how I felt. Deep down inside, I sensed that no one understood me. My requests were unmet, and the doctors grew weary of my constant defiance. Some days I took my aggression out on my family, which brought them to tears. When I needed a bedpan, I did not want to follow protocol and wait on the nurse. If a family member were present, I preferred their assistance to a stranger. My mother did not understand this, and with each request insisted that I call a nurse. On one occasion when my need went unmet, I looked my mother in the eyes and whispered, "Get out." My sisters tried to intervene and explain the rationale behind my mother's decision. Unwilling to listen to their explanations, a hand gesture followed this request, suggesting that I did not want to hear any further discussion.

This treatment was unbearable for my mother, who, without hesitation, relocated to Orlando to commit to the recovery of her second child. She silently stepped away from my bed in tears, disapproving of my behavior but unwilling to offer a reprimand. My mother did not recognize her daughter sitting on that hospital bed. I was lashing out on anyone who overlooked my requests. Most days, I resorted to tears whenever my body throbbed with pain. No one was accustomed to the weakened and confused Faith I had become. I am usually the backbone and strength of the family. Like a sponge, I would absorb everyone's pain and convert it into rays of hope. Now I stood in dire need of divine intervention, as I felt forced to cope with this unfair hand dealt along life's journey.

The nights in the step down unit were long and cold, and I could not imagine a minute without the presence of my family. Whenever I acted out in frustration, it was because of the inability to communicate my needs. I was hurting, but no one could reach me; confused, and no one understood me; needy, but no one could satisfy me. I did not want to be alone; I just wanted someone, anyone to console my aching heart. There were times when I requested that my family stay instead of leaving to conduct much-needed business. My mother laughs about this today, but I specifically requested that she return from her errand with my black Chinese shoes. These shoes are very similar to bedroom shoes because of their comfort. I wanted to wear these shoes during my stay. She did not bring the shoes, but this request confirmed that I was regaining my capacity to remember.

## Tragedy Has No Face

There were no mirrors in my room, and I had seen no reflection of myself since the car accident. I recall lifting my right hand, only to touch what felt like matted hair on my head. I not only lost control over the functions of my limbs, but my hair turned on me as well. I left nothing to the imagination. I requested a mirror immediately! Nothing could prepare me for the much-anticipated reflection that waited. The little black mirror finally arrived, and my mother and sisters gathered around the sides of my bed. This was indeed a vital moment for me, when I would discover how bad it really was.

I held that mirror up to my face and was horrified at what I saw staring back at me: this was not my face. I looked like something out of a horror flick. My left eye was blackened and sore. I had a huge scar from the top of my head that traveled along the left side of my jaw line. There was a second cut, which aligned perfectly with my laugh line on my lower left cheek. I could not help noticing the huge lump on the upper left side of my head. A small portion of hair on the left side of my head shaved, revealing the stitches. My left ear was torn and stitched back together. My mother did not give me an opportunity to indulge in self-pity. "They are just scars, my dear, and they will heal soon," she whispered.

I took a deep breath and continued with my examination. Since the removal of the cast on my left arm, I noticed the stitches on both sides. I later learned that my entire left arm went through the car window. This explained the severe pain that I felt every time I would rest this elbow on my bed. I took the mirror to view my left elbow, which resembled a pink brain. The car glass ripped through the skin of my entire left arm, and the bruises were still tender. My self-esteem plummeted. Despite the reassuring words of my mother, I was utterly disgusted with what I saw. No part of my body had gone untouched. I wanted to scream, "Why!" I despised the mirror for revealing this truth that I was not ready to confront.

I did not know it then, but this painful, yet necessary examination was the beginning of my healing process. If you ever experience an episode of this magnitude, there will be an opportunity on your journey to recovery when you must come face to face with your tragedy. This is the painful part. Tragedy has no preference; I realized that if this could happen to me, it could happen to anyone. No one wants to accept that a situation so horrible and devastating could ever happen in his or her lifetime. Life will throw you a blow that you may feel ill equipped to handle. It may take weeks, months, or even years to accept your altered lifestyle. Once you have dealt with the harsh reality of your tragedy, an opportunity to accept and embrace your situation will arrive; easier said than done, I know. My opportunity did not arrive during the first few months, but I decided to take baby steps until my time for healing arrived.

That night, after inspecting my body, I cried myself to sleep. The most devastating thoughts that echoed in my mind during the midnight hours were, "God allowed this to happen to me," "I didn't do anything to deserve this," and "I am a monster." This particular thought haunted me for an entire year: "No one will ever want someone with a broken and marred body." My insecurities became evident, and eventually I did not care for visitors - apart from my family members. I viewed my guests from a different perspective. Now when people came into my room, I knew what they were viewing. I paid close attention to my visitors' faces as they glanced over my scars. Some people could not resist staring at my scars once they thought I was not paying attention. These visits only heightened my self-awareness and dissatisfaction with my condition.

It took a few days before I decided to get off the pity train and do something about my perceived self-image. I could not change my altered physical appearance, but I was determined to regain my self-esteem. I requested the services of my personal beautician and hair stylist, Sherrina, a friend and colleague who stopped in with no hesitation. She stayed for several hours, fulfilled my request for cornrows, and treated my hair. I figured that I would start light. Once she finished, I looked into my little black mirror and was pleased with what I saw. A few days later, I contacted my friend, Tekoa, and requested that she arch my eyebrows. Tekoa was speechless after hearing that I was able to speak. She, too, came in, but she was a little nervous because she did not want to injure my frail body. She put her heart and soul into perfecting my eyebrows. Once Tekoa was finished, I held the mirror to my face and almost recognized the reflection that stared back.

# CHAPTER FOUR

## Torture Of Therapy

### Preparing for Rehab

**D**uring my final week in Orlando Regional Medical Center, I received a visit from Nurse C, a representative of Lucerne Hospital. Nurse C stopped by my room to deliver the great news that I would be transferring to the rehabilitation facility. She was very excited and impressed with my progress. She assured me that the rehabilitation process would be an essential component of my full recovery. With intrigued ears, I listened to Nurse C as she explained the tasks that lay ahead. Rehab would present the challenges of re-learning such basic skills as feeding, bathing, and self-dressing.

On July 1, I completed a swallow study. I passed the test, which cleared me for regular diet while seated at 90 degrees. I was looking forward to feeding myself, but I feared my stomach's reaction to regular food. The trauma associated with the car accident caused the development of stomach ulcers, resulting in a partial gastrectomy. I only had 20 % of my stomach remaining, and I was amazed at the limited portions that satisfied my appetite.

I was excited about the opportunity to bathe myself, but I feared the frightening task of re-training my bladder. The accident left me with a ruptured bladder, and for the previous two months, I had grown accustomed to the Foley catheter. Haunted by the thoughts of wetting myself during rehab, I feared the worse. Nurse C continued to explain my daily schedule, which would include eight hours of intense physical and occupational therapy, scheduled psychological analysis, group aerobics, and routine doctor visits. Nearing the end of her long list, Nurse C paused and glanced at my face for a response. I offered my sincerest reply, "That is exactly what I need." I went on to list all of my qualifying credentials, totally ignoring the fact that I was involved in a serious car accident. I shared with Nurse C how I started as a personal trainer and insisted that I knew first-hand the hard work and commitment necessary to reshape your body. I made a bold confession, "I have done it before, and I can do it again." Nurse C listened with a smile and politely shook her head in agreement.

I seized the opportunity to revisit my glory years. As I reflect on this behavior and others similar in nature, I realize the degree of isolation that I experienced during my hospitalization. I desperately wanted to regain my spot as a functioning member of society. I felt, act, and dressed as a patient during the first two months at Orlando Regional Medical Center. I just wanted Nurse C to know that there was much more to me than what she currently witnessed lying in bed. These are the mental repercussions of a trauma victim. There is a never-ending struggle to regain your sanity in the eyes of those who witnessed your struggles and knows your weaknesses.

My family acted as my legal guardian during

my most critical hours. Just prior to my acceptance into Lucerne Hospital, my family consulted my preference of rehab facility. I was given the option to return to Palm Beach County or remain in Orlando. I held my goals close to my heart, and I knew I would eventually get back on track with my life. I chose to remain in Orlando to finish what I started. It is of the utmost importance to allow recovering patients an opportunity to recover their hopes and dreams. These visions and dreams will fuel the desire to get back into the fight of life. Reminiscing on that visit, I am so glad that Nurse C did not laugh at me or crush my dreams with words such as "no," "impossible," "never again," or "I don't think so." The words that you speak during these times are so crucial because they can either uplift or demolish one's self-confidence.

Once I completed my list of reasons why this transition into therapy would be the best change for me, Nurse C kindly reminded me that rehabilitation would offer challenges unlike anything I had ever experienced. She told me that sometimes I may have to cry my way through therapy, and at times I may feel like giving up - but giving up is not an option! Those words seared my heart that day and echoed throughout my final days at Orlando Regional Medical Center.

I remember the first time I assisted with giving myself a bed bath. The washcloth alone was a task to maneuver. I was surprised at how weak and frail my body had become. Just sitting in an upright position with the slightest bend caused tiresome breathing. My family and nurses were there to remind me of the difficult tasks that awaited me in rehab.

# The Transition to Rehab

My friends decided to stop by for a visit during my last few days in Orlando Regional Medical Center. Once everyone gathered into my room, I shared the exciting news about rehab. My friend, Chrystol and I were teachers at the same school. She expressed everyone's love and well wishes for my recovery. As Chrystol spoke, I could not stop staring her in the face. I subconsciously thanked her for the greetings as my mind went back to the restaurant. Chrystol was at the restaurant with us the day of the accident. This thought triggered the beginning of a thought pattern that would lead up to my memory of the car accident. I cannot explain why I did not pursue that thought with a few follow up questions. I guess I was too excited about leaving for rehab, or perhaps it simply was not the time to go down memory lane.

The day had finally arrived. My family had been in my room the night before, packing up my personal items and arranging my outfits, my alternative to those hospital gowns. I was transported via ambulance to Lucerne Hospital a few hours into the afternoon. Upon my arrival, I was surprised to discover that I was a candidate for the special rehabilitation program, the Brain Injury Rehabilitation Center, also referred to as the BIRC unit.

The paramedics wheeled me to my room, elevated my body off the hard stretcher, and carefully placed me on the bed of my new residence. I am almost positive that Nurse C was aware of this accommodation, but after my speech on how great I used to be, she probably did not have enough time to give me the full details about the actual rehab facility. After my brief tour, I concluded that this floor was indeed not the place for me. I observed a man wearing a metal helmet speed walking down the hallway. I could not help overhearing the cries of a patient who was about two doors down from my room, sounding like he, too, did not want to be there. On the first day, I mentally began to count down my stay in the BIRC unit. I instructed my body that we had exactly one month to get it together. It was a little scary at first, but I was determined to make it work.

I met the entire staff during my first week in rehab. This team of professionals included Dr. B, my nurse, occupational therapists, and the physical therapist referred to as "Sergeant." After my tour of the facility and review of the weekly schedule, I was convinced that I was up for the challenge. The nurse confirmed that during rehab, medicine was not administered through an intravenous tube but would be available in pill tablets every four hours.

After a long day of introductions and patient orientation, the pain had already taken effect. That evening, after settling into my hospital room, I was totally convinced that my success would be dependent upon my ability to endure - and not succumb to the pain. The next morning, my rest was interrupted by a knock on the door. The door slowly opened, and I glanced at the clock with the aid of the hallway light. It was about five o'clock in the morning, and I was in no mood for guests. It was the first of my daily visits by my doctor and his assistant. Dr. B first inquired about my well-being. He then went on to conduct a routine check of my wounds, feedings, and medications. My weight was a big issue. I had lost 40 pounds since my car accident, and, no matter how I tried, the weight kept pouring off. Although my doctor placed me on a regular diet, this did not help because I regurgitated every meal. Dr. B encouraged me to eat as much as I could to prevent further weight loss. This requirement only deepened the stress of meeting the demands of rehab.

# The Torture of Therapy

My doctor ordered that I was to be non-weight bearing to the left wrist, but could weight bear through the left elbow. Weight bearing was tolerated to my upper and lower right extremities. My first task during my stay in rehab was learning how to get into the wheelchair from my bed. I realized the severity of my injuries once I engaged in physical activities. My muscles were completely fatigued, and I had to rely on the strength of my right side to maneuver my entire body. The practice of standing up and sitting down in the wheelchair triggered unbearable pain. I felt helpless while lifting my body off the bed. I was relieved after each session because, once the therapists left, they took the torture with them. I converted my room into an obstacle course. I kept the wheelchair at the right side of my bed to practice the transfer process.

For my second assignment, I had to come up with measurable goals to accomplish before exiting the program. There was only one thought that came to mind: I wanted to experience 110 % recovery in every area of my life. My sister wrote this goal nice and bold on the white board, beside my schedule. I enjoyed the company of my family, and I disliked the rule that forced them to leave by 10 o'clock each night. On the other hand, I am sure that they were grateful for the rest.

Every part of my body ached, and the pills just could not ease the pain. The earliest I could receive pain medicine was every three hours. After just two hours, my body was throbbing, but I had to hold out for another hour. I reminisced on my days at Orlando Regional Medical Center, particularly how easy it was to push the button and request a shot of morphine. During the late night shift, one nurse in particular was faithful to every call. He would come rushing in at the first sound of the buzzer. He simply prepared the needle for injection, selected the appropriate vein, and injected the medication. Shortly after the injection, I was relieved of all the pain. The absence of morphine was a harsh transition for me, and at times, I thought it was unfair. The doctors had no idea the degree of pain that my body was still enduring. Pain pills just did not work for me. As I progressed towards my goal of 110% recovery, the struggle and pain met me with greater intensity.

In-between occupational therapy, physical therapy, and aerobics, my doctor recommended at least four hours on the CPM machine for the left knee. This machine bent my knee from 0 to 60 degrees, with an increase of 5 degrees when tolerated. I despised this machine because it only caused more incurable pain. Nurse C was right: during the first week alone, I cried myself to sleep every night and threatened to give up during the physical therapy sessions.

I received my third task within the second week. I had to practice walking with a left upper extremity platform-rolling walker, one that would relieve the pressure from my left side and permit me to walk on my own. I mastered the task of getting out of bed and into a wheelchair. Now, it was time to walk. My therapist instructed me to lock the wheelchair and stand up while gripping the modified walker, without using my left side. After struggling to stand up, I finally strapped my right arm onto the walker. My task was to hop using the walker from my bed and into the hallway. I thought to myself, "How hard can this be?" A sharp pain through the palm of my hand accompanied the grasp of my right hand on the handle of the walker. Once I gathered enough confidence, I released a hop. There was about a three-minute pause before the second hop because I had to soak up all of the pain. "Unbelievable," I thought. I had gone from jogging two miles every morning to struggling to take a second hop. Tears began to roll down my face as I heard the still small voice of Sergeant in my ear saying, "Count it all joy."

My second hop was accompanied by a surprising outburst, which was loud enough for everyone to hear me, "My hand is hurting!" The echo that followed caused my anger to kindle even more as Sergeant insisted, "You can do it." I can do it; this carried no weight from a person who was not in my position. I translated that message as, "Get on with it, you cry baby." I made it to my tenth hop and requested to end the session. As I wheeled myself back to my room, I felt defeated and angry at the world. This was a new level of frustration, and I did not see the purpose for such torture. I felt as though I was exchanging one injury for another.

The next day, after breakfast I went to the group exercise session. I could not do much besides arm curls and leg extensions on the right side of my body. The room overflowed with injured patients, some unable to do anything. I remember a particular patient who came in with his wheel chair. He wheeled over to grasp the exercise bars, elevated his body off his chair, and carried himself across. I looked down and was surprised to notice that he had no legs. I left feeling inspired and guilty at the same time. There I was crying about my condition - which would improve with time - and here was a man who had no opportunity to use his legs. I later discovered that a truck crushed this man's entire lower body, and the doctor had to amputate his legs. This taught me a valuable lesson: when you feel you are at your lowest point, someone has it even worse.

I remember an episode during an exercise session in the hallway. I was unable to walk and grew frustrated with the pain associated with hopping on my right leg. I decided that I just could not do it anymore. Mentally, I had given up. The tears began to roll down my cheeks as my lips trembled with pity. I broke down in the presence of the therapists and the entire front desk of the BIRC unit. As I took a deep breath to give in to defeat once again, I heard a prevailing voice that uttered these words of encouragement, "The race is not given to the swift, but to those who can endure." It was my therapist, and she was committed to the completion of my session. Almost instantaneously, I pulled on everything within me and decided to move forward. I took a deep breath and released a hop. Despite the pain that I felt, I was determined to finish, and eventually I did. This was a mile marker on the journey towards my recovery. On this day, I decided to embrace the pain. I was determined like never before to endure the torture of therapy and push through to a promising future. I kept a journal of my continued progress.

- Reach Maximum potential and to recovery 110%

- 1st - I walked 10 ft w/ the walker

- 2nd - I walked 24 ft w/ the walker

3rd - I walked 55 ft w/ the walker

4th - I walked 95 ft w/ the walker

5th - Today I walked 115 ft w/ the walker
    Thank You Jesus!
6th - 215 ft. today!

# CHAPTER FIVE

## The Devastating News

July 21, 2006, marked the day that I would receive the most devastating news of my life. On this particular day, I was very energetic. I became familiar with the facility and enjoyed spending time with the other guests. It was late in the morning, and I did not have my therapy. I wheeled myself down the hallway to review my schedule. I made a stop by one of my favorite person's rooms. This woman was such an inspiration to me. She was a schoolteacher for decades and served as a principal before the accident that landed her in rehab. She knew my story very well. In fact, after hearing my story, she discovered that her son performed one of my surgeries. Her son, who is a doctor at Orlando Regional Medical Center, placed the filters in my leg to prevent possible blood clotting. The next day, she brought her son to meet me, and I thanked him for a job well done.

As I wheeled back to my room, my social worker stopped me in the hallway and informed me that there would be a scheduled meeting in my room shortly. I noticed the block for the meeting on the schedule earlier that morning, but I did not give it much thought. By the time I got into my room and transitioned onto my bed, I noticed the door gradually open. It was my mother and sister, Michelle. They greeted me with a kiss and a hug and brought two seats closer to my bed. I was thinking to myself that something was about to go down, and I perceived it to be a serious matter.

Michelle came closer and informed me that they had to talk with me and were waiting for my social worker to arrive. Shortly afterward, my social worker poked her head in the door and asked if she could come in. She came in and stood to the left side of my bed with my family. Then all eyes were on Michelle. I took a deep breath, afraid of what I might hear.

Michelle began the conversation by refreshing my memory of my repetitive questions regarding the accident. I had no idea where she was headed with this, but by the look on her face, I knew that I had to listen intently for the next few seconds as she gathered her thoughts. She started by saying that two boys were with me during the accident. The look on my face was one of disbelief. My sister continued to explain the occurrence of the accident. One of the students broke his arm during the accident, and the other student died from the impact. Before my sister could finish her sentence, I released a deep mourn and burst into tears. "No! No! No, Michelle!" I yelled at the top of my lungs. "Why?" I demanded to know which one died. My screams vibrated throughout the entire room when I learned the fate of my student.

I struggled to sit up in my bed. This could not be happening to me. I asked my sister again, to make sure that I was not dreaming. My mother and the social worker both grabbed my hand, but this degree of pain refused comfort. "It's all my fault," I said aloud. The level of guilt that I felt was unbearable, and I was willing to accept the repercussions of this tragedy. I could never replace this precious life. I recall asking my family the resounding question that would haunt my thoughts for the remainder of my stay in rehab, "Why not me instead? Why did God have to take the baby?" I felt powerless and disillusioned. I just wanted to be left alone to grieve the loss of my precious "godchild."

The mourning ceased for a moment, but I rehearsed the saga once those memories came rushing in. Disheartened and confused, this was my routine for the next few days. I could not sleep, I did not want to eat, and the only reason I attended therapy was to get my mind out of depression mode. Too many emotions to deal with, I broke down during therapy several times, and for a brief period I could no longer participate. I appreciated my therapists for respecting my wishes, because at that particular moment I was not very receptive to outside comments. My mother has a saying, "He who feels it, knows it." Unless you have personal experience with this level of trauma, it is very unlikely to come up with the right words to say. I believe that during these times it is sometimes more beneficial to listen rather than speak. We know that everything will eventually be all right. We just need the opportunity to vent as we face the harsh reality that it is NOT okay now.

## Anger Phase

*In contrast to the stage of denial, this stage of anger is very difficult to cope with from the point of view of family and staff. Anger is displaced in all directions and projected into the environment, at times almost at random. (Kubler-Ross, 1969)*

I began to experience this phase of anger in the step down unit at Orlando Regional Medical Center. I am not proud of this particular phase of my hospitalization because the people I love and care about had to experience a helpless, very frustrated, angry, and impatient patient. I shared with you the times that my mother had to leave my room in tears because of my attitude. I have a good relationship with my mother; she is my best friend, and I can talk to her about anything. What hurt her most was that she was limited in her ability to understand my speech and bear the pain inflicted by the accident.

I remember before one of my major surgeries, as my weak and frail body lay on the stretcher awaiting transport to the operating room, I signaled for my mother to stand by my side. My mother held my hand and leaned in, as I whispered in her ear, "I don't think I am going to make it." I cannot explain the discomfort associated with those words of doubt. Even though I had every right to feel that way, I still chose to maintain my level of faith in the midst of adversity. My faith was constantly under attack. Once you have given up mentally, with no one to pull you out of your despair, you lose the fight. Tears swelled up in my mother's eyes as she struggled to swallow the fear and doubt. She grasped my hand tight, insisted that I not speak such words, and reassured my spirit that I was going to make it. Those words of faith resonate in my heart to this day. It was weeks before my mother recited those words to another soul. She refused to release doubt into her heart. Only a strong and faith-filled mother could bear this struggle.

In the midst of adversity, the ones you love suffer the most. Unfortunately, the person who is trying to deal with an altered lifestyle may inflict the suffering. If you ever encounter a trauma victim, it is most beneficial to both yourself and the individual if you attempt to place yourself in that person's shoes. Try to understand, rather than take offense or respond out of pity. The last thing I needed was for someone to stand over me and shed tears about how horrible my condition appeared. That is why I appreciated my family and friends, who refused to allow any negative energy into my presence.

Allow me to summarize the extent of my transition: I had gone from achieving a great degree of success in my career, I was an innovative and respected educator who was on the brink of completing a series of published writing with my students. I was in the last semester of my master's degree at Stetson University. My personal life blossomed with trusted friends and a great deal of spontaneity and fun. In less than a few seconds, I was stripped of all that I worked hard for and lay at the mercy of God, my doctors, and the countless electronic devices connected to my body. Anger kindled in my heart whenever this unfair situation came rushing to my mind. I would use body gestures to get my point across to anyone that would listen. What I yearned for was far greater than food, bed baths, and routine checkups. I wanted answers for life's unjust dealings.

### Dealing with the Grief

The grief caused by this unfortunate outcome was unbearable. I knew that for the rest of my days I would never forgive myself for allowing this to happen. I blamed myself for the premature death of this child. At that time, I still did not have the full understanding of the circumstances surrounding the accident. I felt the burden for both families and could not imagine how they were coping with the situation. My sister informed me that the funeral was a week after the accident. When I asked what caused his death, I was afraid of the response. I was horrified to hear how he died. I felt like I was in the center of a horror script, with no possibilities of a happy ending. For a brief moment, I felt deceived by my own family members and friends, who chose to exclude me from this important information. For two and a half months, everyone who entered my room was advised not to bring up the circumstances surrounding my car accident. I received no phone calls, and the television avoided the news stations. "His mom doesn't blame you Faith," my sister would reassure me. She did not have to blame me because I blamed myself. My family told me that the aunts of my godchild came to the hospital during my time in the Intensive Care Unit to offer their condolences and prayers. His aunts wanted me to know that they did not blame me for the accident. They expressed their joy in knowing that their nephew shared his last few hours on earth happy and with the one he loved, his favorite teacher. This brought me comfort, but I would grieve this loss for months to come.

On June 21, 2006, before I went to bed, I prayed my own prayer of serenity and asked the Lord to help me get past the pain, frustration, depression, and the struggle with blaming myself. After that prayer, one thing was clear: I could not change what had already happened. I vowed that night that some good would come out of the tragedy and that the memory and name of my "godchild" would live on forever. I recorded this news in my journal:

I was in a car accident on
May 24, 2006. I injured my
left side. My left leg broken,
pelvis bone crushed and replaced, left
arm broken. In addition my right
leg heavily lacerated and lastly my
stomach was cut open from top
to bottom.

# CHAPTER SIX

## The Life Of Job

If asked to recap my tragic experience in a mirror-image synopsis, only one daunting figure comes to mind: Job. I dedicated time to read the book of Job one month prior to my car accident. A compelling voice in my heart led me to that book. I did not understand it then, but the life of Job would encourage me through all of my turmoil. My mother made this connection with the life of Job and my condition during my stay in the Intensive Care Unit. She stood over my bed, empowered to speak these words of encouragement: "Daughter, God is going to bless you just like He blessed Job - and even greater." Unable to respond to these words, I humbly nodded my head in acceptance. I recall stealing away into a quiet place of my apartment during the silent hours of the night, digesting every aspect of the book of Job. I paid close attention to Job's disposition, mental stability, and I empathized with his calamity. Somehow, I connected with Job, this man of great prominence, one who God bragged about and bestowed great honor. I immediately connected the favor of God that was upon

Job's life with the favor of God that is upon my own life.

If you are not familiar with the story of Job, allow me to take you through the journey of how one man's decision to trust God in the midst of his tragedy ultimately led to his triumph.

The book of Job is located in the Old Testament amongst a group of books referred to as Poetical or Wisdom. Job was a man who lived in Uz. He was honest inside and out, a man of his word, who was totally devoted to God and hated evil with a passion (Job 1:1, MSG). The economical measure of Job's wealth surpassed that of all the men in the East. He owned seven thousand sheep, three thousand camels, five hundred yoke of oxen, five hundred female donkeys, and many servants. In addition to his economic status, Job was happily married with three beautiful daughters and seven strapping sons. Job had it going on, and he knew it.


## The Believer's Faith


According to the book of Job, chapter one, verse six through twelve, Satan seizes an opportunity to ask God's permission to afflict Job. In his conversation with God, Satan states, "What do you think would happen if you reached down and took away everything that is his? He'd curse you right to your face, that's what." Through careful observation of Job's behavior, Satan was convinced that Job's prosperity was a direct link to his happiness. You see, Satan concluded that the only reason Job flourished was due to the protected blessings of God over his life, his family, and his business endeavors. Satan's ultimate scheme was to manipulate Job into thinking that his heavenly Father, his provider, his mentor, his financial advisor, the one who brought him up from nothing and made his name great throughout the land, his God - with the very same hands that blessed him - would turn around and curse him.

Satan would love nothing more than to see faithful, obedient, and righteous children of God such as Job lose the one thing that secures their relationships with their heavenly Father: their faith. Without faith, it is impossible to please God (Hebrews 11:26, KJV). Throughout the bible, we witness the believer's faith used to access the supernatural intervention of God in situations when human abilities reach their limitations. We refer to these occurrences as miracles. When a Centurion realized that he was incapable of healing his servant who suffered from paralysis, he called on Jesus to speak a word of healing. The faith of the Centurion impressed Jesus, who announced, "I have not found so great faith." (Matthew 8:5-10, KJV).

I believe that faith is a spiritual key that grants us access to experience the extraordinary blessings and favor of God, while living out our purpose and calling on this earth. "Have you noticed my friend, Job? There's no one quite like him—honest and true to his word, totally devoted to God and hating evil." (Job 1:8, MSG). During His conversation with Satan, God's boasting on Job proved that He trusted Job's ability to maintain his faith in the midst of life-altering circumstances. God obliged the tempter's request to touch Job's possessions. God instructed Satan that under no circumstances could he touch Job's life.

## The Testing of Job

A normal day in the life of Job consisted of feasting and fellowship with family. One day, Job's children decided to take the fellowship to the home of the eldest brother. Some translations refer to this particular day as the birthday of the eldest son. Job remained home, unaware and ill prepared to combat the whirlwinds of life. Moments later, a series of disastrous events claimed Job's livestock, material possessions, and children. After each unfortunate episode, the only surviving servant returned to Job's home to report the loss.

There you have it, Satan's first attempt to shake the faith of God's servant, Job. As he looked on with immense satisfaction and convinced that his plot worked, Satan was astounded to witness the faith of this great man rise to the occasion of worship. Yes, you read that correctly. Job's reaction to this series of disastrous, heart-wrenching, and faith-testing events was to fall down and revere the one who blessed him with it all. I am sure that Job indeed experienced a degree of insanity. It is recorded that he first ripped his garments, shaved his head, and then bowed down to worship (Job 1:20, KJV).

I can only imagine the various thoughts that bombarded Job's mind. Job recalled the times when he rose early in the morning to offer burnt offerings unto the Lord - not for his own sins, but for those of his children. He considered how he lived such a holy and righteous lifestyle, abstaining from the very presence of evil. Moreover, imagine the onlookers who witnessed the firsthand account of this great man stripped down to his bare bones. Job had no one to turn to but God. "Not once through all this did Job sin; not once did he blame God" (Job1:22, MSG).

During this crucial time in his life, Job was in

dire need of medical attention to help soothe the boils that eventually covered his entire body. Job required emotional condolence to help him mourn the loss of his children and to maintain some form of mental stability. Job was not alone; he and his wife were both survivors of this catastrophe. When life was at its worst and Job was down to nothing, his own flesh and bones, wife, helpmeet, and mother of his deceased children advised him to curse his God and die. Its one thing to face such an immense degree of hardship, but to face it alone by the default of your loved ones has to be excruciating. There is an age-old saying: "What does not kill you will make you stronger." Unfortunately, the faith of Job's wife came to a screeching halt as she chose to surrender in the midst of adversity. The hardship was far too great for her to endure.

Isolated by the storms of life, Job mourned the death of his children, scraped his boils with a potsherd, and tuned out the noise of his critics as he pled with God to grant his death wish. Have you ever taken a minute to pause and try to fathom one day in the life of Job? Oftentimes we stand and gaze at someone else's situation and wonder, "How in the world do they do it?" Better yet, "…if that were me, I would…" I made this same observation as I read the book of Job. I strained to understand how a human being could undergo such insolvency and still maintain a level of sanity and faith. The human race does not have a clue as to what we can endure with the intervention of God's grace. Rest assured, your day of adversity will come; but as long as God's grace is present, you are empowered to overcome. In God's mind, Job already had the victory; it just took forty-two chapters until Job realized this for himself. Job had to arrive at a place of acceptance before he could experience victory.

# The Testing of Faith

Not only is my name Faith, it is my trademark. I can relate to Job when he took it upon himself to pray and offer burnt offerings unto the Lord on behalf of his entire family. Somewhere along the line, we have lost this fervor and passion to reach out to the lost and dying, including those who are members of our family. I remember a time in my life - and still today - when I would not cease to pray for the deliverance of my entire family. Endless nights while under the roof of my parents' house, I would awaken around midnight and meet God in the living room for a one-on-one prayer session concerning the issues that plagued my family.

Every trial that I have experienced and will experience in life brings me closer to understanding the magnitude of God's faithfulness. On the afternoon of May 24, 2006, my life was left in shambles and my light surrounded by darkness. This tug-of-war with death was overwhelming, but the news of the life taken was even more devastating. There I was in the Intensive Care Unit, in a medically induced coma, enthralled with pain, and stomach cut open from the top to bottom. My family waited on the doctor's report, each time their faith shaken with more news of medical complications. Surgery after surgery, doctors advised my loved ones to prepare for my death. When the doctors gave up hope, the only one that my family and friends could turn to was God.

As my body lay on the hospital bed, my eyes remained close and swollen from the impact of the accident. My tears were the only response to let my family know that I was attentive to their presence. On one particular day, while the songs of worship ministered to my spirit, I waved my hand in worship unto God. My family gazed in amazement as they read my lips, which uttered, "God, you are awesome." Tears streamed down my face as I worshipped. This declaration confirmed that my faith resided in the only one who I acknowledged as my redeemer.

It is important to understand that not everyone is designed to withstand the trials and testing of life with you. Some things you will have to endure alone. Count your blessings for the few that will stand with you. Job learned the hard way, "My brethren are far from me, and mine acquaintances are verily estranged from me. My kinfolk have failed, and my familiar friends have forgotten me," (Job 19:13-14, KJV). I was astounded to hear and see the degree of support that came from my family members, friends, church members, colleagues, community members, and nationwide prayer chains. My automobile accident aired on news stations throughout the state of Florida for weeks. The update of my condition traveled fast with the assistance of the latest technology. There were friends and family members who chose not to visit me during my most crucial hours. The person who I admired and respected stood over my body in the Intensive Care Unit and swore that I would require medical attention for the rest of my life. In his eyes, my condition was too far-gone, and a miracle would never become reality.

Like Job, my life was in disarray, my body utterly broken, and I remained at the mercy of the almighty God. To the naked eye, I was already defeated. If your doctors have given up hope, whom else can you turn to but God, the giver of life? I learned well after my recovery that another individual declared, "She will die and not live." Talk about disappointed! I could not believe that these words escaped into the atmosphere to land into the hearing of those believing God for a miracle. Tragedy can shake even the greatest of faith. If you choose to consume your mind with doubt, this obstructive weapon can destroy your precious faith and ability to endure during the time of testing.

As my body continued to bounce back, I still had to deal with the day-to-day repercussions of surgery. I remember the day finally arrived for the removal of suture bands that held my stomach together. The doctors had to pull and tear the bands out of my flesh. I cringe to this day when I consider the unbearable pain. I cried and begged for mercy, but the doctors reminded me that this procedure was necessary. After the doctors exited the room, I prayed silently, requesting that the Lord take my spirit. I felt as though my body could not sustain any more pain. For a brief moment, I forgot that I had already survived the worst. Sometimes it is difficult to look past your present hardship into a brighter future. The trials of life will attempt to paralyze your faith, but with the support of others, you can push towards complete recovery.

My mother constantly used Job's life as a reference for what God is capable of doing for me. She reminded me of Job's triumph and God's blessings upon his life. It is easy to read and learn about this experience, but to encounter such a tragic event yourself is unexplainable. Using someone else's experience as a road map will encourage and refresh your spirit, but the instructions that are tailor made just for you will be released during the journey. Until then, you have to endure the struggle and make a conscious decision to win the fight.

# Go Ahead and Vent

Job undergoes emotional meltdowns throughout his encounters. Job's days were filled with anger and grief, "Obliterate the day I was born. Blank out the night I was conceived! Let it be a black hole in space." (Job 3:3, MSG). As he complains to God about his problems, his friend, Eliphaz, rises to the occasion and encourages him through the struggle. Eliphaz reassures Job that the blameless people have never been completely wiped out, neither have the honest people been destroyed. In spite of the encouragement that his friends provided, Job found himself giving room to bitterness and resentment, "I can't stand my life—I hate it! I'm putting it all out on the table, all the bitterness of my life—I'm holding back nothing." (Job 10:1, MSG).

In chapter three, The Torture of Therapy, I shared with you my frustrations with my doctors and therapists. The tasks of regaining my strength and training my entire body were overwhelmingly difficult. I survived each session, mostly in tears, but it was not until my release from rehab (almost three months after my accident) and my entry into outpatient therapy that I realized a deep root of bitterness targeted my soul. This emotion surfaced with my daily struggle to complete the simplest routines around the house. I hopped from my bed to the bathroom, my ankle inflamed with pain. The distance from my bedroom to the living room felt like a mile. I appreciated my sister, Michelle, who took time out of her life to relocate to Orlando and help me get on my feet. I tried to appear strong in the presence of my family members, who were constantly present to offer their assistance because I did not want to be a burden.

My family suffered enough, so instead of giving them anything else to worry about, I would shut my room door and complain to God about my chronic pain, limited mobility, ongoing guilt and frustrations. Unable to kneel down at my prayer table, I would sit at the edge of my bed and bawl in pity. I made sure that the music was loud enough to drown out the noise of my sobbing. The sorrow was heavy and the burden was great. I was frustrated with the world, God, and the person responsible for my present condition. I yelled into my pillow, "Why! What the fu** did I do to deserve this?" At the end of each plea, I asked God to speak to me and say anything. I just wanted to know that He was near. On the other days when I confronted God about my injuries, I reminded him of His son, "None of His bones were broken; how could you allow my bones to be broken?" For a short period, this bitterness distanced further communications with God.

It was in the presence of my mother that I felt the most vulnerable. Whenever she was in town, and it was just she and I, the tears just came streaming down. Most times, there were no words, just sobbing. My mom would sit and listen, allowing me to cry while she massaged my swollen ankle with alcohol and whispered a prayer. She would begin by saying, "Faith, you have to talk to God and tell Him all about it." I felt like I was at the end of my rope with God. I already knew what He was going to say, and at that point, I could have cared less to hear from Him. All I wanted to know was why He would allow me to endure this degree of suffering. I was not only concerned with myself, but the families of the other victims weighed heavy on my heart. So many people were affected by this tragedy, and for what reason? I could not imagine God's response to this disaster.

If you ever encounter someone who has dealt with calamity, it is important that you take the time to listen to what they are saying and choose your words wisely. It does not matter if the message that they convey is disturbing, just allow them the opportunity to vent. It actually took Job's friends seven days before they were prepared to speak to him. Struck by his travesty, Job's friends decided to get down in the slums with him, allowing their presence alone to furnish support. Not only should you allow a trauma victim the opportunity to release, but also it is also important that you try to understand their pain. Job seized the opportunity to vent, and all he needed was a listening ear. Job knew that God was able to deliver him, but as time transpired his ray of hope darkened as his conditioned worsened to the point that his body was covered with worms and sores, and his skin was broken.

Sometimes, it may look like it is getting worse before it gets better. This is neither the time to give up or give in. You have to give in to the knowledge that you are limited in your ability to deliver yourself from tragedy. That is why in our Father's Prayer we ask that the Lord deliver us from all evil. There are some things beyond our control, and it is during this time that our faith and trust in God elevates to a higher level. This is a supernatural realm, where miracles are performed. Once a human being encounters a state of helplessness and make a conscious decision to activate the faith that is within, we can experience a miraculous deliverance in His will. A miracle can take many forms: emotional, spiritual, psychological, physical, or financial. The method God uses to deliver us is not important, just as long as we realize that it was only by His grace.

# In The Midst Of The Storm

While in the midst of mayhem, my mind reminisced on a signature sermon that my Pastor often teaches on the storms of life. He uses a storm as a metaphor to describe the heartaches and pain associated with the journey of the human race. This message highlights three critical areas in life: an individual is either coming out of a storm, about to enter a storm, or in the midst of a storm (Jackson, 2008).

As I read about the struggles and desperation of Job retold in his forty-two chapter biography, I paid close attention to his disposition during each destructive episode. Distraught, Job did not allow his present condition to alter his faith in God's ability to deliver him. Job convinced himself that if this were indeed the hand dealt by God, God alone possessed the power to restore his life.

The book of James, chapter one, verse seventeen clearly states, "every good and every perfect (free, large, full) gift is from above; it cometh down from the Father of all [that gives] light, in [the shinning of] whom there can be no variation [rising or setting] or shadow cast by His turning [as an eclipse]." Job refused to give Satan credit for his misfortune. God allowed Satan's hands of destruction to move throughout Job's life. What better candidate to endure life's hardship than Job? A man recommended by God Himself. God's word declares that He will not give us more than we can handle. God was confident in Job's ability to withstand the storms of life.

Life is good when everything is going our way. What happens when all that you have worked hard for comes to a screeching halt? The size of the storm does not matter; however, it is important that you maintain your level of faith while in the midst of the storm. A storm can be the destruction of your finances, mental stability, physical health, loss of family members, or even your career, just to name a few. You can rest assured in knowing that even when your present situation and circumstances change, God's love and ability to deliver you does not change.

## Better Is The Ending Than The Beginning

Intermittently throughout his encounters, Job reminds God of his uprightness, "The stranger did not lodge in the street: but I opened my door to the traveler" (Job 31:32, KJV). Finally, the moment arrives when Job hears from no one else but God. God's reply to Job's self-righteousness: "Where wast thou when I laid the foundations of the earth? Declare, if thou hast understanding" (Job 38:4, KJV). In other words, who are we to tell God what to do and how to do it? We are no match for His omnipotence. After constant dialogue with God, Job offers his humble reply, "I know that thou canst do everything, and that no thought can be withholden from thee. Wherefore I humble myself, and repent in dust and ashes" (Job 42:2&6, KJV).

One thing is for sure, the trials of life are humbling experiences. I am a fighter and a very strong-willed individual. With hard work and discipline, I am able to accomplish a great deal of success in my personal life and in the lives of others. This tragedy brought me down to my weakest state of being. I was dependent on God, the machines, doctors, nurses, and family members. I could not even lift my own finger to scratch my head. It was humiliating to lie in my own feces and wait on the nurses to change my soiled garments. I felt embarrassed and knew that once the stench left the room, I was the talk of the hallway.

Like Job, I focused on myself during these crucial hours. The decision to internalize my affliction came subconsciously. I was too weak and emotionally deprived to consider anything or anyone else. I remember when my baby sister came to my hospital room in the step down unit. She whispered in my ear that she was pregnant and asked if I was mad with her. Unable to offer the emotional support that she sought, I simply replied, "No, why would I be mad with you?" My sister and I still revisit this particular conversation and laugh because we both were in dire need of help. It is okay to laugh. Laughter is a medicine that will keep even the weakest heart merry.

Now the finale: God turns Job's captivity around. In the final stage of his storm, God instructed Job to reach out and pray for his friends. This may have been a difficult task because if anyone required prayer, surely it was Job. The book of Job, chapter forty-two, verse ten states, "And the Lord turned the captivity of Job, when he prayed for his friends: also the Lord gave Job twice as much as he had before." The story goes further and states that the Lord blessed the ending of Job more than his beginning. Job's family restored, he gained a greater economic status that he lived to enjoy until he was 120 years old. The life of Job is the very epitome of triumph! The way that he endured his hardship as a good solider is a great example for those who have dealt with tragedy, presently in the midst of tragedy, or will endure tragedy.

# CHAPTER SEVEN

## Hopes And Dreams Deferred

*For I know the plans I have for you, plans to
prosper you and not harm you, plans to give you
hope and a future. (Jeremiah 29:11,
NIV)*

### God Speaks

With every passing day, I regained strength
and anticipated my release from rehab. The doctors
and nurses were constantly complimenting my
progress, and I knew that it was only a matter of time
before I received that visit confirming my departure. I
remained busy, doing anything that would keep my
mind out of the danger zone. There was a constant
battle in my mind, and most days I found myself in
the victim's corner. "Was this car accident my fault?
This may be a character flaw, and my need for self-
acceptance has finally driven me to the edge and
injured those I love dearly." I recited the five words,
"It is not your fault," often spoken to me by my
mother and sisters. I convinced myself that they were

only trying to ease my guilt. My soul tormented with guilt, I vowed that I would never again be involved with another child's life. This was my only answer to an unexplainable situation, complete and utter avoidance.

My thoughts drifted to the lifestyle of Job and the occurrences he experienced. I know that God is sovereign and that He alone possessed the power to prevent Satan's intervention in the life of Job. The saying, "What was meant for your bad, God would turn it around to work in your favor" comes to mind. The only problem was that I could not imagine any good from this turmoil and strife we call life. The residue of tragedy was undeniably visible. Every time I inspected the damages done to my body, all I could think about was that God allowed this to happen to me. Forced to sip from this bitter cup, I despised every bit. I had my days of triumph and experienced moments of defeat. My emotions felt like they were on a roller coaster ride. I tried my best to contain them, but like a fountain they came pouring out. Some days my family just stood in silence, while their presence alone offered strength. I was beginning to feel guilty, not only because of the accident but also for the stress that I witnessed my family endure. In every possible way, I tried to relieve them of the stress that the accident imposed on all of our lives. During each visit, I tried to put the best foot forward, only to suffer the consequences later. At times, I had to encourage myself, "Weeping may endure for a night, but joy comes in the morning."

My desire to walk again manifested in my dreams and I saw myself back in a place of productivity and strength. I would wake up from these dreams because of the sharp pain that raced through my knee, ankle, and lower abdomen. I spent many restless nights in rehab, and at times my body would automatically awaken to the cold silence of the room. After sleep escaped, I stayed up only to ponder my existence in this world. I finally shared these experiences with my pastor, who encouraged me to use this time to speak to God. I was a bit negligent at first, but obedient to the curiosity of His responses.

The one person I neglected to consult concerning my situation was awaiting my invitation so that He may speak. After several nights of chilling silence, I heard in my spirit, "I took you through this because I knew that you could recover. Most people have gone down this path and did not make it, but I knew that you would." I recorded these words of hope on the pages of my journal that I would revisit weeks later. Mentally, I began to put the pieces together. These were the exact words spoken by the doctors to my family. The first 24 hours are very critical and most trauma victims do not recover. My doctors dubbed me "Miracle." Tears swelled up in my eyes after this revelation, and my perspective towards my present situation changed drastically. I considered it a privilege to be a candidate for this journey. My triumph throughout this tragedy brought glory to the name of God. Each time my condition worsened, doctors stood amazed by my constant comeback, and they insisted that my family continue to pray to God.

Despite how bad it may seem, I believe that there is a lesson learned in every storm that we will encounter on this journey through life. The eye of the storm is the most still and quiet place located in the center of very rapid and destructive winds. There is peace in the midst of the storm. If we can just take a moment to quiet our spirits, we can hear His still, small voice declaring that everything will be just fine. God wants to restore, His desire is to heal, and He longs for us to trust and know that He will keep His word.

# Hold on to the Promise

While on the road to recovery, one of the hardest things for me to accept was the deterrence from my hopes and dreams. I convinced myself that delay does not mean denial. No matter what situation or circumstance you are facing, hold on to your dream and do not let it go! Write it down and recite it because when the time is right, preparation will meet opportunity, and your time for success will become reality. Prior to my car accident, I was in the final semester of my master's degree at Stetson University. The educational leadership program is an intensive one-year program that requires tremendous dedication and sacrifice. My schedule reflected an eight-hour class every Saturday and over twenty hours of home-work on a weekly basis. My Saturday ritual resembled a drive to Barnie's Tea and Coffee shop for a 16 oz cookies and crème freezer. Once that craving was satisfied, I hopped into my car and traveled thirty minutes from Orlando to the school campus in Celebration, Florida, for a full day of learning.

I enjoyed the camaraderie that this graduate program offered with other educators. During these sessions, relationships were developed and I felt affirmed walking into my destiny. My dream since childhood has been to become a principal of my own school. Inspired by my elementary school teachers, I experienced the calling to influence the lives of other children at an early age. These teachers went the extra mile to make a noteworthy contribution to my life. Whether it was a kind word, a reprimand, or a lesson taught, there were significant moments when I felt that these teachers genuinely cared.

Every human being is born into this world equipped with special gifts and the ability to make a difference. The ability to impart knowledge and wisdom that will better the lives of others is a divine gift from God; therefore, being a teacher is one of the greatest gifts on earth. My mother identified this gift within me years ago, during my high school career. It was during a church service, while holding a little child in my hand; my mother looked at me and in her own words said that I was going to do something big in the lives of children. Although she could not put my calling into perspective, she did acknowledge the gift. I doubt that my mother remembers even saying these words to me. It was something about those words that empowered me that night as I etched them in the corner of my heart. In due time, that prophetic overtone would set me up for several encounters with destiny.

I was a business major during my first year at the University of Central Florida, but I failed all of my courses miserably. I desperately desired a change. One day, on my way home from class, I decided to take a short cut and strolled through the education building. I paused for a brief moment to read the bulletin in the hallway. A woman who was walking by stopped, stood beside me, and said, "You are a teacher." Surprised by this comment, I looked at her and explained that I was not a teacher, but a business major. She insisted that I was indeed a teacher and that she could see it in my stand. This confirmed the greater calling within that I had to pursue.

I believe that God allows people to enter our lives for a significant reason. The day I decided to revisit my career path, there was a woman positioned to steer me in the right direction. My grandfather and Bishop also recognized a calling on my life. During my senior year in high school, he told me that I was going to preach the gospel to millions of people.

Throughout the painful stages of my recovery, I forced my mind to collect every encouraging word spoken over my life. I chose to trust God in this disastrous event and believe that He was going to allow me to live out my hopes and dreams. God is faithful. He promised me that He would never leave me nor forsake me, so I chose to believe just that.

## Change Your Perspective

After the car accident, my perspective towards the completion of my master's degree shifted to the fulfillment of a spoken word. This word manifested itself as a promise. This promise says that, if I keep the word of God before me as a guide for my daily decisions and actions, I will experience sure triumph and victory. This is the guarantee spoken to Joshua, the successor of Moses, right before he embarked upon the complex task of leading the children of Israel into the promise land. "Do not let this Book of the Law depart from your mouth; meditate on it day and night, so that you may be careful to do everything written in it. Then you will be prosperous and successful" (Joshua 1:8, NIV). With a multitude of both small and great, Joshua faced the difficult task of leading God's people into the promise land. Joshua's success in this great commission was not dependent upon his gift to lead or fight, but his ability to adhere to God's instructions. When faced with his most difficult tasks, Joshua reflected on God's promises to help him maintain his focus. These words offered Joshua relief and comfort in knowing God was with him.

# Get Back on Track

Strategic planning is a necessary survival technique after dealing with any traumatic occurrence. The transition back into reality was a major component of my recovery during outpatient therapy. Honestly, this conversion was the scariest for me throughout this experience. I remember sharing my fears with my sister, Michelle. I was intimidated with the thought of regaining my independence and functioning as a part of society. My therapists and I created problem and solution scenarios. These real world scenarios ranged from physical set ups to ensure mobility, activities to relieve stress, and work-related encounters. In the meantime, I had to undergo physiological examinations to confirm that I was ready for real world activities such as working, driving, and returning to work and school. I felt insulted when my ability to make sound decisions was questioned, but the brain-injured report was something that I could not evade. Fortunately, I passed each examination and my therapist suggested professional counsel only as an option in extreme cases.

A major concern for me was my limited mobility. My left knee burst open from the impact of the crash, and the scar tissues limited my range of motion to only eighty degrees. Sitting down and bending my knee to this limit came with a lot of pain. I had undergone two knee manipulation surgeries during my stay at Orlando Regional Medical Center, and the furthest my knee bent was one hundred forty degrees under anesthesia. I was determined to reach my 110% goal. I also have a metal plate in my left leg that extends to my ankle, which restricts my flexibility. I was horrified when I reviewed the x-rays that revealed dozens of screws holding my bones together. My doctors insisted that the hardware would remain and that for the rest of my life I would have to succumb to a certain degree of joint pain. Despite this news, I looked forward to my transition from a wheelchair to a walker. I thought about my dreams of walking, which fueled my momentum and allowed me to push past the pain. As time progressed, my dream slowly became a reality, and a couple weeks later I was walking with a cane. I kept the walker for a few months until I was able to balance and walk at a good pace on my own.

My greatest obstacle during this time was getting behind the steering wheel and driving again. Six months had transpired since the accident, and I was not looking forward to driving. It was hard for me to accept that I feared driving because my passion is to travel. Road trips are therapeutic for me, and I use this time to regroup my thoughts and relax. My current condition required that I hire a driving service to escort me to my therapy sessions. Those forty-five minute trips to the therapy sessions seemed like forever. I was okay once I found the drivers who were able to deal with my screams of terror and uncomfortable body gestures during the trip. Deep down in my heart, I was not satisfied with being a passenger for the rest of my life, but I was too afraid to venture back onto the highway behind the driver's seat.

If you have to start from ground zero before you can get back on your feet, do just that with a smile. I had to learn how to trust those around me with my life. My therapist prepared me to conquer one of my biggest fears: returning to the highway. First, I had to commit several visits to prepare for the clinical driver assessment, which involved hours of studying and re-learning the basic driving skills. On October 31, 2006, I completed a behind the wheel assessment. Prior to this huge venture, I dedicated my mornings to constant meditation and recitation of faith-filled confessions. I recorded these words in my note pad, recited them in my mind, and wrote them large in black mascara on my bathroom mirror. On the day of the driving test, I felt a sense of peace reassuring me that everything would be just fine. I scored high in the areas of operational and performance skills, resulting in the full reinstatement of my license. Now that I could drive, I was on a conquering streak.

# CHAPTER EIGHT

## From Tragedy To Triumph

*Weeping may endure for a night but joy comes in the morning… (Psalms 30:5, KJV)*

### Endurance is the Key

Growing up, I have always admired certain individuals who possess the ability to influence the world, such as Dr. King, Rosa Parks, John F. Kennedy, and Oprah Winfrey, among countless others. These individuals have what we refer to as "charisma," a divine gift of leadership with the ability to awe the masses and inspire loyalty and commitment. These individuals did not arrive overnight. Before experiencing the sweet taste of triumph, they learned how to overcome the bitter taste of tragedy.

Apostle Paul, one of the most prolific writers of the New Testament, speaks from personal experience; his words designed to empower his readers. In the book of Romans, chapter five, verses three to five, he states, "We can rejoice, too, when we run into problems and trials, for we know that they help us develop endurance. And endurance develops strength of character, and character strengthens our confident hope of salvation. And this hope will not lead to disappointment." Endurance in this text refers to the ability to wait in hope. No matter what you are going through, if you can just endure to the end, life occurrences will mold you into a better person. I venture to say that God is allowing you to be shaped into purpose. Sometimes, situations can get so bad that it may appear as if God has forgotten about you, turned His back on you, and for some, you probably blame God for your troubles. Just know that if God allows you to meet head-on with tragedy, He will enable you to last! The key to your triumph is your ability to wait in hope and trust that God will see you through to the end. How you choose to wait is important. Consider that in the midst of the storm there is peace. Once you calm your spirit and fine-tune your ear to listen, there will be a life-altering message designed to bring you through the storm. Conversely, if you choose to fight against the winds and the waves, the currents of life will draw you out of peace and thrust you into a state of chaos.

After enduring months of guilt and depression, I made a conscious decision to wrap my arms around this experience and embrace the lessons designed to make me a better person. This decision became the pivotal point in my recovery. No longer was I satisfied feeling like the victim. Instead, I decided to conform to a champion's mentality. This transformation offered a difficult challenge. Rather than giving in to the pain, I fulfilled my physical requirements with a smile. I became the victor. It was only a matter of time before this very attitude would manifest itself in my day-to-day activities.

# Dr. Martin Luther King, Jr.

Dr. King was born 1929 in Atlanta, Georgia, referenced as one of the best southern cities for blacks to live in (Haskins, 1977). He recognized at a tender age the call to enter into ministry and join the ranks of leaders to guide the protest for social justice. At the age of 19, his father, Reverend Martin Luther King, Sr., pastor of Ebenezer Baptist church, ordained King a minister. King completed his doctoral studies at Boston University by the age of 25. He and his wife, Coretta, relocated to Montgomery, Alabama, one of the most segregated cities in the South. Dr. King felt a strong passion to aid in the civil rights movement and better the conditions of his people.

Before Dr. King could ever envision the mountaintop, he had to make it through the harsh realities of racism and segregation, lonely nights in solitary confinement, and lead thousands of followers in months of boycotting and sit-ins. Dr. King's vision of freedom gained great notoriety by other public officials, such as President Kennedy, Jesse Jackson, and numerous pastors and congregations. On April 4, 1968, around six o'clock in the evening, the words that Dr. King uttered to his wife Coretta five years prior became a reality: "I don't think I'm going to live to reach forty" (Jackoubek, 2005). Dr. King was assassinated on the balcony of the Lorraine Motel in Memphis, Tennessee. In spite of a tragic death, Dr. King's legacy continues to live on in the hearts of millions. Dr. King received hundreds of rewards during his life, including the Nobel Peace Prize in 1964. His birthday is recognized as a national holiday, and his children continue to uphold his banner of peace and equality. The spirit of Dr. King lives on, and this is triumphant!

# Oprah Winfrey

Oprah Winfrey was born on January 29, 1954, to the parents of Vernon and Vernita Lee Winfrey. By the age of four, Vernita Lee could no longer care for her daughter and handle the demands of work and childcare. Therefore, she decided to leave Oprah with her grandmother, Hattie Mae, and join the millions of African Americans in the great migration to the north and Midwest. Alone under the strict rules of her grandmother, Oprah was reared in the church and encouraged to read, write, add, subtract, and memorize scriptures before kindergarten (Weston, 2005).

Before Oprah could gain the title as the wealthiest and most powerful American woman in the entertainment industry, she had to survive the hardships of growing up poor. Oprah was raped at age nine by her cousin and suffered numerous sexual encounters at the hands of her closest family members until the age of fourteen. Switched from home to home, by the age of thirteen the young and then promiscuous Oprah was pregnant and embarrassed. After a devastating miscarriage, Oprah took this as a second chance to refocus and gain control of her life. Oprah began by breaking barriers as the first African American Miss Fire Prevention in 1971. She was a recipient of numerous academic awards and began work as a news broadcaster on an African American radio station.

The twenty-three year old broke ground with WJZ-TV, an ABC affiliate, and landed her first talk show, "People Are Talking" with co-host Richard Sher. After her acclaimed role as Sofia in "The Color Purple," several Emmy awards, the passing of the Oprah bill (a national child protection act), and countless accolades, Oprah still strives to make a difference. Her recent triumph is the Leadership

Academy for girls in South Africa, to which she has donated $10 million.

So, what brought these great individuals to a place of thriving success? I am sure that their ability to endure hardship played a significant role in their eventual triumph. The driving force behind your transition from tragedy to triumph is your ability to endure. Endurance refers to your ability to last, continue, or remain (Merriam-Webster, 2006).

## Become A Pillar Of Hope For Others

During my time in rehab, there were patients constantly in and out of the Brain Injury and Rehabilitation (BIRC) unit. Still experiencing a great degree of pain, I was adamant regarding the opportunity to motivate the new patients. There were times when my physical therapist insisted that I make my way out of my room and visit other patient's workout sessions. Even though she did not state her reasons for encouraging my unannounced presence in the group workout sessions, I sensed that she noticed my ability to motivate and inspire others. She was calling the innate leadership within me that was forced to take a back seat to my tragedy. Before rehab, I had grown so accustomed to people telling me what to do that I did not recognize the freedom of making my own decisions. After gathering enough confidence, I finally decided to branch out and share my experiences with others.

I immediately identified with a new patient who suffered similar injuries. I sensed her fears and frustrations while completing the exercise moves during our group sessions. The therapists gave me several opportunities to conduct the workout sessions, and I began each segment by sharing my car accident, past struggles, and current progress. After my demonstrations were complete, this particular woman volunteered to demonstrate the exercise. Without hesitation, she hoisted her injured body up and out of the chair as she struggled to stabilize her balance on the modified walker. I empathized with her as she strained with tears in her eyes to complete each activity. I understood the aggravation associated with retraining your body, and, like my therapists, I was there to encourage her every step of the way. I arrived to a place in my journey where I did not harbor all of my emotions to indulge in self-pity. Instead, I channeled my energies into helping others develop their inner strength. My mind reflected on the life of Job, and I did not realize this then, but I was slowly turning around my captivity. That which threatened to destroy me now torched an internal flame to help others live again.

I realized that my story gave others hope. I was the biggest cheerleader for the other patients, and, most of all, their inspiration. An elderly woman named Juanita told me that my story would bless thousands of people across this nation. I was humbled and honored to hear those words, which reminded me that this tragedy would soon become a testimony for the world to both see and hear.


## On The Road To Victory

There are many inspirational moments associated with this experience. I was out one night, weeks after my release from rehab, shopping for a flat screen television with my sisters. During this time, I was still using a walker and a wheelchair when necessary for shopping. Upon our return home, I braced my frail body in preparation to exit my sister's car. I froze, paralyzed by a sharp pain that ran through my left ankle. I took my aching right hand, held tight to the car door, and lifted my body out of the car. I made a faith-filled confession that night as I struggled to regain my balance, "It will not be like this always." From the corner of my eye, I could see my sisters staring at me with pity in their eyes. Michelle immediately chimed in and agreed with this faith-filled confession. I have come too far on this journey to look back now. Pity could not reside for long because my faith rose to the occasion. I immediately felt the power of these words lift the spirits of all those who were around and showered us all with hope and comfort.

I had to submit to the process if I wanted to experience triumph. Yes, there were times when I literally wanted to stop, throw in the towel, and call it quits - and I did a few times. I realized that giving up was not the answer. Refusal to perform an exercise routine during physical therapy was not hurting my therapist; it was setting me a step further from reaching my target goal of 110 % recovery. This determination drove my passion to experience a fulfilling life. This time around, I vowed that I would not only live a new and resurrected life, but that I would live life to the fullest. The year 2007 gave birth to my new motto, "Live life to the fullest and have no regrets."

## Living Life With No Regrets

Shortly after my release from rehab, my home became my office, and I worked expeditiously on the completion of my students' chapter books. I established a publishing company, Children's Heart Publishing, for the sole purpose of producing the work of the young and gifted writer. This became my personal project, a positive way to channel my energy and alleviate my worries. Most nights, I fell asleep with my laptop opened to a chapter. I shared a connection with these precious stories, the experiences of these students, and their perceptions of the world around them. After several contacts, I retained editors, professional reviewers, and a professional artist who made these books come alive. I was excited about the new book project and ways to promote the creative work of these young authors.

On November 10, 2006, I decided to make my motto reality. My dream truck is the Toyota 4Runner, and, after several failed attempts, I walked into the dealership and drove out with my new salsa red truck. I cannot explain where this confidence came from, but I knew that it was my time to have the desires of my heart. On my way home, the picture of my crushed Honda Civic flashed across my mind. I drove my truck home in tears that night and gave all praises to God. The effect of the accident was losing its sting, and that night I felt triumphant.

## From Tragedy to Triumph

I made several visits to my place of employment to meet with the students and share the good news of their published books. During my trip to the school, I had to pass the scene of the crash. This was the first time I had passed the area since my car accident. There was a memorial placed on the side of the road with a picture of my "godson." This experience was difficult for me, and I cried on my way to and from the school. In the middle of a meeting with the principal, while sharing the good news about our student's books, I broke down into tears. She consoled me, and commended my strength and courage.

After talking with her, I realized that I had an extensive amount of healing; the pain and the memories were still fresh. Sometimes, you have to go back and confront hurtful situations before you can move towards a promising future.

I returned to Stetson University in the summer of 2007 to complete my master's degree. Three months transpired since my release from outpatient therapy, and I was on target with my goals. My expectations were higher, and I was willing to do whatever it took to make it all work. I could not predict my psychological stability, so I decided to take a risk and register as a full time graduate student. This time around, the courses were more challenging, and at times, I doubted my ability to maintain my sanity. I felt exhausted after a couple hours in class, and it was difficult focusing during the group activities. The physical transitions presented a challenge because of my limited mobility. Sometimes the pain was so great that I could not walk on my ankle; I had to resort to a slight hop. My professors and colleagues were very understanding and accommodating, but did not want my condition to deter the focus of the class.

I caught myself mentally drifting in and out in the middle of the lectures. I fought the tears when my mind reflected on the tragedy that had occurred just one year ago. After a couple hours, my metal plates were stiff from the chilled room. At times, I had to excuse myself for a bathroom break and limp my way to the door. I immediately became the center of attention, which was embarrassing. I constantly reminded myself that it was an honor to be present once again among my colleagues. Even though most of the times they stared in pity and sorrow for my obvious pain, I believe they shared the same honor.

The triumph continued, and two months later on July 24, 2007, my students and I celebrated our first book-signing event, hosted at Borders Bookstore. It was a monumental event for those children, their parents, the school, and community. Those published authors enjoyed being celebrities for a few hours as they autographed their individual books. The community banned together to support our efforts, and that night we sold over one hundred books. The fulfillment that I experienced at the completion of that project was unexplainable. I harbored the stories of these children in my soul, and I was not going to rest until I gave birth to their message. I was the proudest person in the world.

The summer was winding down, and the start of the new school year was just around the corner. I had several interviews for the position of a reading teacher. After three years at the middle school level, my initial goal was to transition to the high school level. I desired this exposure to aid my future placement as an administrator. My counselors and therapists advised that I return to a familiar setting to avoid stress. After much thought and consideration, I convinced myself that the time for change was now. Since August 2007, I have worked as a high school reading teacher in the Osceola School District.

My return to the classroom offered its challenges. My ankle was still off limits to extensive walking and required elevation and icing daily. I walked equipped with my painkillers to offset the pain. I literally cried for the first few weeks after a full day's work. I was exhausted after walking the entire campus, and 75% of the time, I found myself instructing class while leaning on a desk or a stool for support. I explained my condition to my students, and they assured me that they understood. In the past, I was intimidated about teaching high school students. I was surprisingly confident with my new position because I knew that I had much more than reading strategies to offer these young adults. I felt authenticated because of my life experiences, which made me a spokesperson for life's lessons. Every day that I walked that enormous campus, I would take a moment to thank God for the journey. On my way home from work, I was satisfied with my decision to live the triumphant life.

"Live life to the fullest and have no regrets" is such a strong statement. That declaration became the driving force behind my renewed sense of living. I graduated from Stetson on December 15, 2007. After I passed the Florida Educational Leadership Exam, I entered the "administrative pool," which recognized my status as a potential candidate for an open administrative position within the school district. I became proactive in taking the necessary steps to fulfill my destiny. I had broken free of the bondage inflicted by the three months of hospital confinement. I was experiencing success on an entirely different level, one that bred confidence, and I felt like I had nothing to lose. By the grace of God, I had conquered the greatest enemy to the existence of humanity: death.

In January 2008, I began my doctorate program at Nova Southeastern University. Seven months after my return to the classroom, my high school students and I completed, "Through the Eyes of a Poet." This book of poems highlights 60 of the most talented writers in Osceola County. The school hosted a book-signing event to honor the accomplishments of these gifted writers. What I am most proud about is that the students decided that they did not want to pocket the money from these book sales. Instead, they applied the knowledge gained from our second semester book study and decided that the money should go to stop the genocide in Darfur.

Oftentimes, I find myself looking back on the tragedy and wondering if there were anything I would change. There are over a dozen thoughts that come to mind. I realize that I cannot change my past, but I can proclaim my future. Nothing can ever prepare you for life's misfortunes. Most importantly, after the storm you still have to cope with the residual effects. How you choose to deal with the aftermath is up to you. As for me, I have decided to accept the things that I cannot change and pray for God's grace to make up the difference.

It's okay to remember; go ahead and look back, just make sure that you don't get stuck and soak in the sea of regrets. The decision to turn your tragedy into triumph will prove to be the most difficult decision that you will ever make, but it has its rewards. It is difficult because the conscious effort to push forward despite circumstances is more challenging than retreat. In the end, your reward is the satisfaction of knowing that you are a survivor and you made it despite the odds. There is an immeasurable satisfaction when you decide to take the journey less traveled and choose to turn your tragedy into triumph. No one can do it for you, so I urge you to do it for yourself - starting today.

# CHAPTER NINE

## Reinvent Yourself

*Therefore, if any man be in Christ, he is a new creature: old things are passed away; and behold, all things are become new. (2 Corinthians 5:17, KJV)*

### Look Beyond the Scars

**A**fter outpatient therapy, my desperation for a new look became obvious. The phrase "Old things are passed away" speaks about yesterday's tragedy. I inspected the scars that covered my body daily, most of the time in tears. There is a scar or bruise on every part of my body. I purchased numerous products with promises to minimize the appearance of scars and give them a softer look. I massaged my scar tissues and applied every technique that my therapists taught me. I researched a plastic surgeon and scheduled a free consultation. Unfortunately, the risks sound greater than the benefits. After realizing there was nothing that I could do to remove the scars, I decided to change my outlook. These scars I once viewed as horrendous and dreadful, were now precious and beautiful. These scars told a story of courage and triumph. As painful as my scars appeared, I built up enough confidence to wear clothing to reveal my story.

I recall countless episodes during my usual stroll through the mall; people would stop and glance at my scars, while others looked in utter disgust. There I was, every day of my life reliving the pain and embarrassment of unwelcome attention. In reality, I felt like a patient all over again. I could not avoid the stares. My insecurities did not hesitate to kick into overdrive, "Look at me: obviously a young woman who suffered from a very bad accident. My clothes clung on my thin body and exposed my frail bones. I had to rely on a walker for balance and support. My ankle was literally swollen twice its size, and I had to make frequent rest stops to accommodate the pain." I felt like a spectacle for the world to see. I fought with my subconscious thinking and had to remind myself of my journey to where I am. This is a difficult road to travel, and the world has to look beyond my scars and see the beauty within. I have developed a great sense of humility and honor. The months of enduring the hardship somehow developed patience. I am more appreciative of my family and friends. The compassion that I have to witness others succeed at life's challenges is sincere. I have become a better person. I want the world to experience the new me.

## True Beauty Lies Within

I have naturally fine hair, but after the numerous surgeries, I was amazed at how thin my hair appeared. In addition to a small portion of hair that was shaved due to stitching, I had a huge lump on the top left side of my head. Unfortunately, I developed bedsores, which left two very large and noticeable bald spots on the back and right side of my head. I scheduled a hair appointment with my hair stylist during the first month of outpatient therapy. She was very accommodating and did not schedule anyone in the shop during those hours. I sat in the chair as she worked her magic. I left the salon that day with my spirit lifted. Although I was not where I wanted to be, I was on my way. I learned valuable lessons throughout this entire ordeal. I realize that true beauty lies within a person's heart, and not on the outside. We spend a lot of time and money designing an outward image and neglect to develop the character within. Your true character will show up in the tough times during life's journey. Do not be alarmed when a part of you that you assumed disappeared finds an opportunity to resurface. If this occurs, invest time and energy to produce a positive change. Do not feel bad if the currents of life leave you with a residue. These marks are proof that you are a survivor. For me, these are my scars. My spirit preserved, and I am fortunate for that, but I acknowledged that everything else needed work.

My frequent trips to the mall were dedicated to my quest for a new look. There was an inward change that I wanted to demonstrate in my outward appearance. I was forty pounds lighter and required a new wardrobe. Now I had a choice to make: I could talk about the bones that protruded through my skin or I could find clothing that would compliment my smaller physique. I decided to reinvent myself and embrace a new attitude. The strategic planner in me kicked in, and I rehearsed my story of survival in my mind for anyone who dared to ask: "If you only knew my story, you're looking at someone who has survived death." Each time I did this, the embarrassment that I felt when people gazed quickly dissipated, and I was overwhelmed with self-confidence. I experienced this nobility every time I shared my story with the world around me. I now walked with my head lifted high. I remember one particular occurrence while I was in Office Max shopping for supplies for my student's books. A woman walked up to me and said, "Excuse me, I don't know who you are, but I just wanted to tell you that you are very beautiful." She continued to say that it was evident that I had been through a lot in my life, but it did not matter because God loved me. Affirmation is so very important, especially following a tragic event such as the one that I experienced. Almost two years later, and those words still carry me through moments of doubt.

## Reinvent Yourself

The renewal of the mind, body, and soul is a daily process. You may as well reinvent yourself while you are at it! Seize the moment to create a new YOU! You may have gone through the fire, but you are coming out as pure gold. This is a more refined, pure, and rich state of being. I do not know about you, but this screams authenticity, worth, and honor. What may have caused you misery will now be used as the platform for your service to others presently faced with a similar situation. It was hard for me to focus on this aspect during the first three months of my hospitalization. This did not stop others from encouraging me with these very words of restoration into my hearing and constant meditation.

I meditated on the positive side of this tragedy. My scars, which were once ugly and unbearable to see, now became my glory and the very essence of who I am. I cherished life to a greater degree, and the little things did not even matter anymore. I felt grateful when I made it from my living room to the bedroom after countless hops. No longer would I anticipate the encouraging words of others to get me through the day. I woke up every morning with a positive confession to start my day. While looking in the mirror, I declare daily, "I am destined for greatness," "I am a beautiful woman," and "This, too, shall pass." The most important thing is that I believe what I say. These words were uplifting during my transition from rehab to outpatient therapy and eventually back into the real world.

I knew that confidence was mandatory if I were going to return to the classroom, pursue personal relationships, and accomplish future goals. I purchased an entirely new wardrobe designed to compliment my new size and affirm my spontaneous attitude. I revisited my hair stylist and convinced her to style my hair in an entirely new look. I wore my hair natural for an entire year. I received more compliments with this short cut than any other hairstyle. My confidence skyrocketed after this new look and I drove my new truck in style, windows down, wanting the world to feel what I felt: newness! I felt like the world was at my disposal and that I deserved every good fortune that awaited my arrival. After numerous stomach surgeries, I was concerned about my ability to have children. My doctors assured me that my womb would be okay, which reaffirmed my future as a mother.

Post rehabilitation is an era of transformation for anyone who desires to regain his or her spot as an active citizen of society. Most importantly, during this time, I took time out for me. I invested in the things that I enjoyed doing or simply wanted to do. I was not rushed by time; rather, I allowed time to take its course and live in the moment. Everything else would take care of itself. Each day, I purposed to shine brighter than a shooting star. This renewed attitude showed up in my conversations, appearance, and relationships. I did not hesitate to spend time with family and friends; in fact, the more I occupied my time with self-fulfilling tasks, I avoided depression. There were times I yearned solitude and did not desire to interact with others. On those days, I gave in to selfishness, closed the door of my chamber, and released my thoughts on paper. Poetry became my sweet relief, and I found healing in the lyrics that emerged from my soul. At that point in my life, I avoided stress and welcomed freedom. Deep down in my heart, I knew that I was arriving at the point that I required closure. Before moving forward, there were wounds that were in dire need of healing. I prepared for the day of closure that lay ahead, and I was confident that my time had finally arrived.

# CHAPTER TEN

## CLOSURE

*Being confident of this very thing, that he which hath begun a good work in you will perform it. (Philippians 1:6, KJV)*

### One-Year Anniversary

The wounds that I bear could not be any deeper. My heart ached at the very thought of meeting my godchild's mother. How could I face the woman that this child loved so much, especially when I still blamed myself for his death? What would I say? Not only that, but how would I say it? All these questions and dozens more plagued my mind daily. It had been almost one year since the tragic episode, and I had made countless efforts to contact the mother of my "godchild." After several unsuccessful attempts, I could not help wondering if this were indeed a sign. Maybe if I made contact with his family, I would experience a greater degree of pain associated with rejection and guilt. I was not sure how I would say I was sorry, but I knew that I had to share the last words of this precious child with his mother.

It was the day before the anniversary of the accident, May 23, 2007, and I decided to take one more chance at bringing some degree of closure. I took the phone and dialed the number of the state attorney who represented the victim's family. While the numbers dialed, I took a deep breath and said a soft prayer. I am an optimist, but in this particular situation, I did not know what to expect. Mentally, I prepared for the worst. I coached my heart to hear the words that I dreaded: "It's all your fault." I would offer no rebuttal; only a sincere apology, if given the opportunity. The telephone rings were abnormally long, and just before I decided to hang up and try again the greeting of a woman's soft voice startled me. I was surprised that the state attorney knew who I was, and, by the sound of her voice, she was very appreciative for the call. Immediately following the cordial introductions, we discussed the first trial date for the suspect in custody for the hit and run car accident. I had only one opportunity to tell him, the judge, and the courtroom witnesses about the many sufferings inflicted upon me because of a series of this young man's poor choices. Later in the conversation, I learned that the person responsible for the death of my "godchild" expressed absolutely no remorse for his actions. If that were not heart wrenching enough to hear, he now referred to himself as the, "Baby Killer."

I learned that the mother of the deceased child wept bitterly when she heard the recordings of the suspect's telephone calls made in jail and how he addressed her most precious child. "She was hoping that you would call her, Loretta." My heart skipped a beat, and I could not believe the words spoken by the state attorney. I went on to explain how I made several unsuccessful attempts to contact the family.

To be quite honest, I was not ready until now. The anniversary was a few hours away, and I was filled with hope at the news that EC's mom would be at the site of the accident. Meeting the mother of this talented and comedic young man would be his dreams come true.

## EC's Final Words

The state attorney promised to give me a call with a contact number later on that evening. Evening time could not come fast enough. My heart flowed rivers of emotions, and I knew that, no matter what, I had to share the final words of this precious child with his mother. It was about nine in the evening, and I was in the parking lot of Barnie's Café. I held the cell phone and pressed it firmly against my ear as I awaited an answer while not giving in to the numbness in my legs. Once I heard the quiet, shy voice on the receiving end, my heart immediately felt a connection. "EC talked so much about you, Miss Harris, and I couldn't get him to shut up." We laughed together, and I shared with her EC's last words. In his final hour, EC promised that he would change his life and improve his attitude towards school. During our final hours together, there was something apparently unique about EC's persona. The entire time while EC spoke, I could not help but notice a special glow surrounding his face. I could not take my eyes off him. Months later, another teacher present at the table confirmed that there was indeed a glorious glow on EC's face.

Astounded by what she heard, EC's mom shared the final words that he had with his sister just before leaving for school. The morning of his last day, EC invited his sister to sit at the table, and he offered to share his cereal with her. This attitude was not common for EC because he enjoys eating, his mom continued with a slight chuckle. EC led a discussion with his sister and ended with a request that she take care of their mom. Shortly after, EC exited the front door, on his way to school. EC's sister, surprised by her big brother's request, inquired about her mom's plans. After reassuring her daughter that she did not intend to go anywhere, EC's mom ushered her children off to school.

During both occasions, the attitude that EC displayed was unique, and we concluded that somehow EC knew it was going to be his last day. From the first day of school, EC presented himself as one of my most challenging students. After hard work and patience, I witnessed the evolution that took place in this child's life. During the last nine weeks of school, I witnessed EC grow from a caterpillar into a beautiful and mature butterfly. EC was his mother's first child, and she shared stories of how they learned and grew up together as mother and son. Just as EC and his mom, he and I shared a precious bond, a bond birthed through struggle. It was not until ten o'clock that night in the parking lot that I realized why it was so important to EC that his mom and I meet. He insisted that she and I shared common characteristics. He admired our strength, enjoyed our company, but most of all reserved a special place in his heart just for us.

I was saddened because of the conditions that forced me and EC's mom to meet, but I was honored to have the opportunity to share her angel. Later on that night, we released an inconsolable cry for the premature death of this precious child. I could see where EC gets his strength. In the midst of our tears, between gasps for air, I uttered the words, "I'm so sorry." There was a second of silence, and the words

92

that followed freed me of all the guilt and sorrow that I carried for one year, "Loretta, it's not your fault. Things happen for a reason, and, for whatever reason, God allowed my baby to be with Him. He allowed you to stay so that you can continue to make a difference in the lives of these children." I sobbed even more, but this time it was out of the joy that flooded my heart.

## Closure

I did not know this, but EC's mom said that he would get dressed for school early in the morning just to meet Miss Harris. EC met me every morning to assist with setting up my room. His bright smile and loud voice greeted me at the door every morning as he shared his love for football. I told EC's mom that he vowed to make it big one day just so he could move her into a bigger home. His mom was familiar with the goals that her son had and thanked me for my influence on him. It is amazing how much we can learn from each other. The life lesson that EC taught me is to smile through the struggles. No matter what, never let the passion for life burn out. The last day of school sealed the completion of the classroom book project that my students and I dedicated an entire nine weeks to complete. What began as a classroom effort to capture the attention of my students emerged into something spectacular and life changing. EC insisted that we name one of the characters after him. Mr. C is the name of an office manager who gives a convict a second chance at life. This character exemplifies the very essence of EC, who was a very loving, respectful, and understanding person. You could not stay mad at EC for too long before he would melt your heart with that picture perfect smile and those beautiful dimples. I picture his face as I type. I have never met another so special. We share a bond that will never be broken.

I shared the name of the book with Mrs. B, and she agreed that "Hard Life" is definitely symbolic of her son's life. The next day, we met for the first time at the scene of the accident. EC has such a beautiful family, including his baby brother, who was not even a year old. EC was excited about his mother's pregnancy and discussed their trips to the doctor. Now that his pride and joy has arrived, it hurts me that EC is not here to walk him through the stages of his life. How would this precious baby know of his older brother, who went on to be in a better place?

The media was present at the scene of the accident and requested an interview. I was not in the mood, but I obliged in the hopes of getting the word out about the importance of justice and safety. My mission for the rest of my life is to keep EC's name alive, and I will seize every opportunity to tell his story. The trial was only a few weeks away, and it was time for my voice to be heard. I have a story to tell, and I started with the large viewing audience who witnessed the paramedics remove my limp body from my crashed vehicle.

Once EC's mom and I said our goodbyes and exchanged information, I recalled a video that I recorded with EC's class during a debate on the topic, "Nickelodeon vs. Cartoon Network: Which Is The Best Station For Children?" I informed his mother that the video existed and that I would do everything within my power to retrieve it. After I retrieved the video, I watched it and cried as I viewed the ability of this intelligent young man to light an entire room. I made a copy and sent it to EC's mom, who promised to share and cherish the video.

## Anthony Williams vs. State of Florida

The state attorney's prediction was correct, and the hearing date was postponed for two months. The hearing took place during the fall, after my return to work. I developed cold feet at the thought of meeting the person responsible for my condition and for the death of EC. I knew that it was my civil duty to read my victim's statement. For a brief moment, I had given in to fear. I dreaded the possibility of seeing a family member of the suspect in a local area such as the grocery store. Prior to the car accident, all parties resided in close proximity within the Orlando area. The suspect's younger sister had been my former student two years before this incident. It was reported that associates of the family committed several violent acts against EC's mom following the suspect's incarceration. I feared similar retaliation.

Motivated by my passion for justice, I decided to prepare a victim's statement and address this killer face to face. I wanted him to know the degree of pain I had experienced because of his poor choices and the wounds that will remain for a lifetime. September had arrived, and as I approached the stand to take the oath, I observed the composure of this man: he showed no sign of remorse. I could not feel an ounce of sorrow, or even pain. His eyes were cold as he turned around to observe the courtroom.

I was the first witness called by the state attorney, and I tried my best to answer the questions related to the day of the accident. I have no recollection of the actual accident, only the events leading up to the head-on collision, which knocked me unconscious. When the moment came for me to make my statement, I addressed the honorable Judge directly with faith and confidence:

"May 24, 2006, I remember that day as if it were yesterday. We were returning to the school from lunch, celebrating the accomplishments of two of my star students. Nothing could have prepared me for what lied ahead. Three weeks later, I woke up from a medically induced coma in the Intensive Care Unit, and over a dozen surgeries later, I learned the news that my beloved EC was taken away from us. SUFFERING does not even begin to describe the pain and hardship that my family, close friends, EC's family, and I have endured resulting from the series of poor choices made by Anthony Williams.

The doctors and nurses fought to resuscitate my lifeless body that lied on the operating table. In the meantime, they prepared my family to say their last goodbyes. I sustained a mild brain injury, which tampers with my memory to this day. My left anklebone was crushed and left leg broken. My left hip was broken and left arm took the window, which resulted in a fracture as well. The impact of this vehicle crash burst my left knee and heavily lacerated my right leg.

As horrific as these injuries may sound, my internal injuries were far greater. My bladder was ruptured and liver lacerated. I developed ulcers that caused internal bleeding, resulting in numerous surgeries, including the removal of 80% of my stomach. I have survived by the GRACE of God, the love and support of my family, and life support. All of this caused by one person's choice. We did not ask for this, but are now FORCED to live with the results of your choice, Anthony.

A life was taken prematurely, and hundreds altered forever. We have to spend the REST of our days living with this TRAGEDY, and, <u>Anthony,</u> I believe that you should as well. Your HONOR, it is my desire to see time granted in the maximum of 30 years!"

In addition to my testimony, the judge heard the statements of EC's mother, aunt, and football coach. The judge did not require time to decide the fate of this young man. Almost immediately following the last testimony, it was evident that the fate of Anthony Williams was ready. The Judge sentenced Anthony to the maximum sentence of thirty years in prison. All hearts were resolved and pleased with this sentence. My future as a classroom teacher was at stake prior to my conversation with EC's mom. Making that connection with EC's family truly brought healing to my heart and inspired me to continue and strive to make a difference in the lives of our children. The day that I witnessed justice prevail also gave me hope and assurance that the streets would have one less lunatic to worry about. It is so easy to give up during this journey. Whether you choose to bombard heaven with questions or decide to take the journey less traveled, you must trust the process and have faith that some good will indeed be the product. I strive to be a testament to the truth that, no matter the odds, you can overcome adversity. This excerpt from, "Through the Eyes of a Poet" is my testimony of survival and triumph:

# Overcoming Adversity

I hear noise, but there's darkness all around
What did I do to deserve this vicious fate?
Cold, in isolation and solitude I lay

Why is it that in the midst of the STORM
I feel so ALL alone
The doctors have given up hope
And my family left to cope
With the harsh reality
That tomorrow I might be history

I hear a still small voice that says
Hold my child
Weeping may endure for a night
But, I designed you to withstand this FIGHT

So, I wipe my tears and encourage my soul
With hope that this too shall pass
For He is Jehovah-Shalom and in Him there is no fear
Because through Christ I can, No I will PERSEVERE!

Body utterly broken, but not destroyed
Soul in total disarray, but I'm okay!
Spirit remains untouched
My faith devil you can't shake
Now look at me, here by God's Grace

So when you want to throw in the towel
I pray that these words comfort you in
your midnight hour
It is when you decide to take
The journey filled with Travesty
God will empower you to <u>Overcome your Adversity</u>!


~ Loretta "Faith" Harris

# CHAPTER ELEVEN

## It's Not About You!

*I did not ask for this, but somehow I had proven to
be the best candidate for this journey.*

*~ Loretta "Faith" Harris*

**T**wo years later, after surviving over a dozen surgeries, intensive rehabilitation, six months of outpatient therapy, and enduring long nights consumed with emotional grief, depression, anger, and frustration, I realize that this journey is not about me. In chapter seven, "Hopes And Dreams Deferred," I shared a reassuring word that I heard in my spirit after long nights of silence in the hospital room of Orlando Regional Medical Center. The voice of the Lord said to me, "I took you through this because I knew that you could recover. Most people have gone down this path and did not make it, but I knew that you would." I was baffled by these words. The situations and circumstances surrounding my car accident were so intense that my spiritual capacity to comprehend was distraught.

What makes me different from the millions of people who did not survive the hardship? What sets me apart from the one who waved the banner of defeat in the midst of the battle? What I believe makes me different is my decision to endure the route filled with hardship. It is easier to just give up rather than stay in the fight. Sometimes it may seem as though the more you try to go forward, the more the currents of life pushes you back. When this happens - and it will - do not give up because in due time you will realize that it is not about you! People who love and care for you are depending on you to pull through. I encourage you to think about your future before making a decision to throw in the towel. As for me, I knew that my students were depending on me. I made a promise to publish their books, and this promise kept my mind actively engaged in the fight for my life.

How does one eventually triumph over tragedy? You have to think about the lives of others who are depending on you to make it through the storm. When faced with life-altering circumstances, ask yourself this simple question, "What do I have to live for?" If this question does not generate a list, I want you to close your eyes and picture the world without you. Growing up, I engaged my imagination in this scenario quite often. I would close my eyes and picture a frustrated household. I am sure that it would be hard for my loved ones to get along without Faith, their voice of reason. I was the person my siblings would seek out to speak up against that bully. My mother entrusted me with orchestrating the completion of the household chores before she returned from work. Whenever my father arrived home after a long day's work, he knew that his Faith would massage his aching muscles. If no one has ever taken the time to express his or her appreciation for you, just know that life without YOU is like a puzzle with a missing piece.

My mother always encouraged her children to walk with our heads lifted high because you never know who is watching. I venture to say that people are not only watching but also depending on your lifestyle to teach them a better way. As I mentioned before, the believer's faith is a spiritual key used to access the supernatural intervention of God in any situation. Your faith in action is an opportunity to uplift and encourage countless others. There lived a man whose lifestyle was immaculate, his very presence alone healed and cured people of their ailments and diseases. His ministry restored the hope for a brighter future in the heart of his followers. Thousands of years later, the ministry of Jesus Christ is recognized as the greatest phenomenon the world has ever seen.

## The Commitment Of Jesus Christ

I believe that the life of Jesus is the greatest example of enduring hardship. In the garden of Gethsemane, Jesus experienced His moment of weakness. The book of Matthew, chapter twenty-six, verse thirty nine, shows Jesus falling to His knees and praying out of desperation, "Oh, my Father, if it be possible, let this cup pass from me: nevertheless not as I will, but as thou wilt." For that brief moment, Jesus thought about his sole purpose for living. He thought about how billions of lives would be impacted by His decision to take the journey less traveled. Now, Christianity is the largest world religion, accounting for over 33% of the world's population

(Major Religions of the World Ranked by Number of Adherents, 2008).

The decision to suffer continuous beatings, harassment, embarrassment, and eventually death was not based on the will of Jesus, but that of a higher calling. Jesus spoke candidly about His ministry and purpose, "I come that thou may have life and have it more abundantly" (John 10:10, KJV). The word abundantly means "exceedingly, very high, and beyond measure" (Strong, 1990). Therefore, living the "good life" is exactly what God has in mind for you. "Whatever is good and perfect comes down to us from God our Father, who created all the lights in the heavens" (James 1:17, NLT).

As humans, we are born with an innate compulsion to make sense of the calamity that befalls us. In chapter six, "The Life Of Job," we studied the series of tragic events that occurred in Job's life and the process leading up to his day of victory. According to the biblical account, Job was not deserving of the evil forces that came against him. It is unfortunate that bad things happen to good people. I hope that what I am about to share will help you triumph over your fears of any impending danger. Before any disaster could occur in Job's life, God first had to put His stamp of approval. He gave Satan one condition: he could not take Job's life. Once the agreement was official and the contract signed, Satan went about fulfilling his end of the bargain. How ignorant of the devil to think that he could interfere in the relationship that Job shared with God. When God volunteered Job, He trusted that Job was the best man for the journey. The writer of James says it best, "Consider it a sheer gift, friends, when tests and challenges come at you from all sides. You know that under pressure, your faith-life is forced into the open and shows its true colors. So don't try to get out of anything prematurely. Let it do its work so you become mature and well-developed, not deficient in any way" (James 1:2-4, MSG). So when you are involved in a head-on collision with misfortune, know that you are predestined to overcome. It is a fixed fight!

The prophet Isaiah spoke from personal experience, "No weapon that is formed against me shall prosper" (Isaiah 54:17, KJV). God does not prevent the formation of the weapon (trials, temptations, bankruptcy, failed relationships, or health challenges), but you can rest assured that it will not be successful. How does one measure success? Surely, it is not the material wealth that some associate with success. A rich young ruler came to Jesus and inquired about eternal life. Jesus explained that gaining eternal life required that he deny himself, sell all of his worldly possessions, and give all proceeds to the poor. The young ruler's response to this requirement was filled with resentment. He walked away sad. God told his servant, Joshua, that a great deal of success awaited him but that he had to listen to His instructions. What I define as success is being in the perfect will of God. Doing exactly what you were created to do. Please know that you cannot live a successful, meaningful, and prosperous life in isolation. Relationships are very important, especially during the time of struggle. During my darkest hours, my family and friends unified their faith and petitioned God for my life. Unable to make decisions for myself, my family stepped up to be my voice.

## Take a Stand

Like Jesus in the garden of Gethsemane, the day of adversity can be a very humbling experience. Sometimes God has a way of ridding us of all our selfish pride. Pride is on the "Top Two" list of God's most hated sins. Pride can cause you to spend so much time concerned with your own agenda that you forget about the needs of others. When Jesus resigned His will in the garden, this symbolized his submission to God's purpose for His life. His decision to take the journey less traveled would shape the destiny of the entire world. The writer of the book of Hebrews declares, "Do you see what this means - all these pioneers who blazed the way, all these veterans cheering us on? It means we'd better get on with it. Strip down, start running - and never quit! Keep your eyes on Jesus, who both began and finished this race we're in. Study how He did it. Because He never lost sight of where He was headed - that exhilarating in and with God - He could put up with anything along the way: cross, shame, whatever. And now He's there, in the place of honor, right alongside God" (Hebrews 12:1-2, MSG). When the going gets tough, know that God is with you, and just make the decision to take a stand.

In every situation you face in life, just know that someone has been right where you are. Take notes and learn from that person. If you cannot think of someone with whom you can relate, think of your Heavenly Father. "Now that we know what we have—Jesus, this great High Priest with ready access to God—let's not let it slip through our fingers. We don't have a priest who is out of touch with our reality. He's been through weakness and testing, experienced it all—all but the sin. So let's walk right up to him and get what he is so ready to give. Take the mercy, accept the help." (Hebrews 4:14-15, MSG). Studying the life of Job prior to my car accident helped me to maintain a level of sanity during the storm. I kept telling myself, "If Job did it; I can do it, too." In the end, Job was a wiser and better person, not to mention wealthier. "Though thy beginning was small, yet thy latter end should greatly increase" (Job 8:7, KJV). Keep in mind that your present condition is always better than how it appears. If you stick with it, the finished product will be far greater than you could ever imagine. A certain level of empowerment is associated with a clear vision, "The vision is for a future time. It describes the end, and it will be fulfilled. If it seems slow in coming, wait patiently, for it will surely take place. It will not be delayed. The righteous will live by their faithfulness to God" (Habakkuk 2:3-4, NLT). These are the words spoken by God to the prophet Habakkuk in his quest to find answers in the midst of disheartening situations. During the time of chaos, it was important that Habakkuk envisioned a better future. Your imagination will fuel your passion for a better tomorrow. In the meantime, you just need to focus your lens and adjust your perspective. Every time you find yourself up against all odds, take on a conqueror's mentality. If ever sidetracked, do not stay derailed for too long. Cheerleaders are in your corner, rooting for your complete recovery. We all are entitled to our moments of weakness. It is not how you start the race, but that you finish!

Finally, I want you to remember that it's not about you. You have people who are depending on your very existence. One day, your paths will cross with that of a young girl whom you will encourage to speak up because you spoke up. That young man will thank you for taking time out to encourage him to do better. That single mother will listen to your personal experiences as a single mother more than she would someone who never had that experience. That orphan will know that he or she is not alone. That cancer patient will start envisioning life after chemotherapy. When you make a decision to take the journey less traveled, you triumph not only for yourself but also for that person whose life will be impacted by your story of survival. My mission has just begun, and yours is getting ready to start. Take a stand today that you will live the triumphant life!

# CHAPTER TWELVE

## Testimonials

### Ann Marie Bonner

**F**aith is my cousin, whom I have known for 28 years. I would describe her as loving, caring, genuine, giving, intelligent, as well as a high achiever, great motivator, and a God-fearing woman of faith. I heard about her car accident on the morning of May 25, 2007, at 5:30 am. My mother called me on my cell phone, crying hysterically. The screams were worse than a woman in childbirth. Immediately after hearing the news, my entire body went into a state of shock. I, too, began to scream as I knelt to the floor in my bedroom. I could not imagine life without my dearly beloved cousin.

The sorrow that I felt after receiving the news was more than I could bear. I knew that it would take hours before I could be by my cousin's side, so I instantly started to pray. I spoke to the greatest physician. That physician is Doctor Jesus. I asked Jesus to heal, restore, and nurture her back to health.

Through it all, I have witnessed my cousin go through the valley of the shadow of death. Within the first few weeks after the accident, she was unable to talk, yet I was told that, as the gospel music played, she raised her hands and worshiped God. There were times when she thought she would not make it, but family and friends were there to motivate her to stay strong. The thing I admire most about my cousin was her willingness to restore her body to its full potential and stability. The tasks were not easy, but she kept faith in God and relied on him for her complete healing and deliverance, and He did just that.

Faith's recovery stemmed from her faith in God. Never did she give up, although the roads to recovery were rocky, never did she curse God. Sometimes the pain was unbearable, but through it all, she trusted God. She is here today because of her trust in our great physician, and He has blossomed her into a triumphant woman for all to see. Loretta is a miracle, and my hero.


## Mother Mary Neal

I consider Faith to be my goddaughter, whom I have known for three years. Faith is a strong and responsible individual with a riveting personality. I can honestly say that she is one who truly loves the Lord. Faith has a passion for people, and it is her heart's desire to help others in any way possible. She is an intercessor, one who is in constant prayer for others.

My son, Pastor Andre Neal, told me about the car accident one or two hours after it happened. My daughter-in-law, Valerie Neal, arrived shortly after for moral support. The feeling that came over me is indescribable. The headline of the car crash was the highlight of the evening news. Once I witnessed the news flash, I did not know how to react. I wanted both to scream and faint.

I arrived at the hospital about 6 o'clock that evening, and everyone was in the waiting room of the trauma unit. At that time, Faith was in surgery and in a very critical state. I sat in my quiet corner, praying, and with everything in me, I held back the tears. I dared to believe those words that I heard before I left home, "She shall live and not die."

Eventually the doctors allowed us to see her, and at that time, she was almost beyond recognition. Her body badly swollen, tubes were in her head, and just tubes everywhere! Faith had to endure surgery after surgery. Before leaving that hospital, I had high expectations that God was going to do just what he said. I had not seen Faith for a few days. On a particular day when I walked into the ICU, Faith was laying flat on her back, her hair matted with blood, her eye blackened and swollen, stitches in her face, and a cast on each one of her limbs. The left side was worse than the right. Machines and tubes were everywhere. I recall how Faith's fingernails would always show such beautiful life, as if they were done daily! I never shared it, but that was my sign of living and not dying, freshness.

Faith's mother and I walked into her room together, and she announced to Faith, "Look who is here, it's Momma Neal." Faith looked once, quickly took a second look, and extended her hand to me as tears begin to roll down her face. I walked over to the bed while holding back the tears and gave her my hand. She took my hand, kissed it while moving her head from side to side. As the tears rolled down her face, it was as if she were saying, "Look what has happened to me!" I kissed her and whispered in her ear, "It is okay, you are strong, you will not give in or give up, you are a fighter, and you know the Lord!"

In no time, I learned that Faith was discharged

to rehabilitation. It was during my visit to rehab that I heard for the first time in two months, "Hello Mother Neal." I stood there in amazement and wept uncontrollably. I witnessed a continuous improvement in my goddaughter, and I saw the hand of God perform a miracle in her life. She had to learn how to walk, talk, and care for herself all over again. Faith was released from rehab in a wheelchair that I only saw her use a few times. She went from a wheelchair to a walker to a cane, and from there to complete independence. The first Sunday in September, Faith walked in church in less than four months as a testament of God's mercy. Faith made a conscious decision to turn her tragedy into triumph and take the journey less traveled. She is a mighty woman of God whose purpose is just beginning; many lives' will be touched and restored. I know this was not easy for her and, even in her questions and trying to understand "Why me?" she will understand in due time that it was for such a time as now.

### Pastor Valerie Barr

Faith is one of my favorite nieces, whom I love dearly. I would describe her as loving, full of life, caring towards others, and spiritual. Faith has always inspired me through her preaching and teaching. It was around 10 o'clock that evening when I heard about the accident through Faith's grandfather. After I heard about the accident, my heart skipped a beat, and the space within my stomach immediately felt hollow. After receiving the tragic news, I repeatedly cried, "JESUS have MERCY!" Faith's grandfather and I prayed for a miracle from God. After we prayed for the Lord to intercede, the entire family traveled to Orlando to be near the bedside of my dear niece.

Upon my arrival at the hospital, I was in a state of shock because I did not recognize my niece. Faith was three times her normal size; however, I was able to recognize my niece by her beautiful hands. I whispered in the ear of my niece, "Your mother didn't name you Faith for nothing; the Faith that you have in God will get you through this perilous time." Unable to respond, tears streamed from her eyes down to her cheek. This was confirmation that Faith received my words of encouragement.

Faith's mother and I prayed for a speedy recovery, strength, and for God to restore her from within and out. Today, Faith is a living miracle for everyone to see. It is evident that Faith's fighting spirit brought her back from death's door. Faith is God's child; she is alive and of great triumph because He did not give up on her.


### Sherrina M. Stewart

Loretta and I have been friends and sisters in Christ since 2001. From the development of my friendship with "Key-Lo," she has been consistently honest, nurturing, a burst of laughter, she brings the joy out of the most downtrodden of situations, she goes beyond herself to see you develop beyond what one would see for themselves; she cares and loves you as Christ would love His friends!

I heard about the accident from my roommate, who was working in the records department at Orlando Regional Medical Center. At first, I was in total disbelief, and then I thought to myself, not Loretta, my sister; it is not time for her to leave us, she has so many more lives to help change. I then began to think back on all the times we had in ministry, laughing, and loving life; I proceeded to get angry, and then I started to pray.

The accident became real to me when I went by the scene; my heart ached to see the rubble of what was left of Loretta's car. After that, I threw myself into doing whatever it took to be a blessing to her family, whether by my prayers or just being there for support. There were many days and nights I spent at the hospital in the Burn Trauma ICU; even though Loretta could not see me, I knew her spirit would feel us praying for her. I remember this particular time, Loretta's nurse, who was one of my professors in nursing school, briefed us on Loretta's condition. She was surprised at how well she was improving. She told Loretta's mom and me that she was bleeding on the inside and that they could not find the source.

I did everything to hold back my tears because I knew she was in a lot of pain. Her mom began to stroke her head, Loretta looked at me, and tears began to roll down her face. Her mom and I just started singing songs of worship. I remembered that I had some anointing oil with me, and her mom anointed her and I poured some into my hand. I held Loretta's right hand, her mom held her left hand, and, as we prayed, a peace came over the room, and Loretta began to fall asleep. I was transitioning to move to Miami, and I made an effort to visit with Loretta before I left. By this time, all of Loretta's surgeries were successful, and she moved to a rehab facility. I would do her hair and just chill with her; boy, Loretta had mastered getting up out of bed and doing a lot for herself. With her many scars, she was still bold in her attitude and did not allow anyone to see her feel sorry for herself. I recall a conversation when we talked about her next move. She wanted to move into her own place and finish school. As we reminisced on our good times together, I realized that it was really a miracle of God how fast she recovered in a period of two and a half months.

In April of 2007, less than a year, I saw Loretta at a Women's Prayer Annual Ceremony, where she and I previously served on the Executive Board together. My God, Loretta was looking fierce; her hair was exquisite, she was walking without a cane, still with a little limp, but it was as if she never suffered a car accident. That night she embodied the very essence of beauty; I was so proud of her. She is truly an overcomer from tragedy to exponential triumph!

## Andrea Jackson

I have known Miss Loretta for about nine years. I consider her a role model and older sister. I heard about the car accident a few hours after it occurred. At first, I was shocked to know that Miss Loretta was involved in such a horrific accident. Next, I had to know if she was alright. I tuned into the news for further updates, but the reporter had limited information.

I felt a small sense of relief once I visited Miss Loretta in the hospital, but still a little sad because someone lost their life. That whole night, I was worried because it seemed like every time the doctors said she was going to be OK they came back and said that she might not make it. So, just like the rest of the church members, I did the only thing I knew how to do, and that was PRAY!

I watched Miss Loretta come back to life. I knew that she was a fighter, but I could have never imaged anyone fighting like she did. She fought to live, and live is what she did! Since Miss Loretta has been out of the hospital, she hasn't stopped fulfilling her purpose. In what seemed like no time, she started her publishing company, which in my eyes is very successful. Miss Loretta went back to school and graduated with her Master's degree, which is only one-step closer to her becoming Dr. Harris. To me, her accident was just a stepping-stone for her. God knew that she could handle the storm. He has truly blessed her, and I am blessed to have Miss Loretta in my life.

## Wilhemina Kirt Ford

I have known Loretta for over five years. I am her mentor, and we fellowship at the same church. Loretta is a woman of faith and power; she understands that her life belongs to God. This is why I was upset when I heard about her car accident. I just knew I had to pray and get to the hospital. I remember as I took a step off the elevator near the trauma waiting room, the Holy Spirit whispered to me, "It is not yet her time." I knew at that moment, no matter how she looked or what the doctors and others said, she would recover.

I shared with one of the members how God showed me that Loretta has much more lives she had to touch. She had not completed her assignment, so it was just a matter of time, and she would recover. I also believe that many people will be healed just by her presence.

## Adrienne Jackson

I have known Miss Loretta for nine years. She is a friend and mentor. I would describe Miss Loretta as determined, goal oriented, encouraging, and a teacher. My mother told me about the accident about an hour after it happened. At first, I was really sad and scared. I did not know what to think. I just knew that she was in an accident. I didn't realize how bad it was until I saw her car on the news. All I could do was cry once I learned that her car was totaled.

I went to church later on, and the accident was the talk of the day. The youth were crying, and I, along with some of the older youth, tried to comfort the younger ones. We did the only thing we knew how to do: we prayed. My sister and I went to the hospital after church. Miss Loretta's Family was there, along with her friends and Church family. Everyone was praying for her!

The first couple days, the doctors did not know if she was going to live, but that couldn't stop everyone from praying. Weeks later, she was awake and alert. I was not able to see her, but the people who could gave us updates. Every day, Miss Loretta kept getting better. She kept pressing on and did not let anything stop her. It's like right after she got out of the hospital and rehab she was back on her feet, starting her own business and rock climbing! She is truly an inspiration. She proves that, no matter what man says, if God didn't say it then it's not true. Also, no matter what it looks like, God can use it for good.

**Chrystol Ingram**
**Chrystol Clear Coundz**
**Executive Producer/Founder**
**Orlando, Florida**

I have grown to love Loretta as a friend, sister, and prayer partner for about eight years. I would describe her as one of the most enjoyable people to be in the presence of! She demonstrates the greatest example of resilience for any human being who has suffered from a tragedy, and I greatly admire her strength.

I heard about her accident by watching the news about two hours after it occurred. I was simultaneously notified by the school, at which both of us were employed at that time. After hearing the news, I was greatly devastated, saddened, and afraid - especially after learning of the loss of one of our students. One side of me started to become angry with God for allowing such a terrible incident, but I quickly got over that emotion. Once I received a call from a mutual friend with detailed information concerning Loretta's condition, I grabbed some clothes and headed out the door. I had no idea where I was going; I just felt the need to come to my friend's rescue.

I saw one of the strongest people I know physically, spiritually, and psychologically come to what I believe to be one of the lowest points in her life. She was broken inside and out, literally and metaphorically. Despite all of this turmoil, Loretta found a way to rise to her highest plateau through her faith, as she is also surnamed. Loretta maintained the strength and dignity that only she has about herself.

In less than a month after being released from the rehabilitation center, I called Loretta, just to check on her and see how she was doing. She was very excited, answered my questions, and quickly asked that I call her back because she was driving! I screamed in the phone and could not believe what she had just told me. As tears began to roll down my face, I reflected on her life's journey. I knew in my heart that she would be okay.

**Tekoa Summers**
**Helping Others Pursue Excellence**
**CEO/Founder**
**Orlando, FL**

Loretta is a trusted friend and colleague whom I have known for ten years. She is, without a doubt, a determined, strong-willed, disciplined, and focused individual. I chose these four adjectives to describe Loretta Harris because, ever since I met her, whenever she said that she was going to do something, she would not stop until that goal was accomplished.

Wow! It was like watching a miracle in action. I witnessed Loretta go from not being able to talk and walk to publishing young adult books and hosting a book signing event for inner city youth. Even in the midst of tragedy, I witnessed what I said in the beginning: determination, a strong will, discipline, and focus. Regardless of what the reports said, and despite the timeline that she was given, Loretta had a goal set for herself, and she accomplished it.

# ——— AFTERWORD ———

**I** wrote **The Journey Less Traveled: Choose to Turn Your Tragedy into Triumph** out of a sincere desire to let the survivors of any tragedy know you are not alone. The contents within this book are designed to transcend the reader's cultural barriers, maturity, and experiences. If you have dealt with tragedy, you can relate to the aftermath associated with the storms of life. Likewise, if you know of someone who has survived tragedy, this book is designed to enlighten and teach you how to treat that precious vessel.

No one looks forward to facing his or her day of adversity, but with faith, hope, prayer, and the love and support of close family and friends, you will be equipped to overcome. There are key steps and strategies that I pray you find helpful during your personal journey through life. Keep this book in a safe place and allow the words written to encourage you to take a stand!

I would love to hear from you and learn how this book has affected your life. Please take a moment to visit my website: www.chpublishing.org.

Also, send a friend request to MySpace page: www.myspace.com/chpublishing.

Sincerely,

Loretta Harris
Post Office Box 691223
Orlando, FL 32869-1223
**Website**: www.chpublishing.org
**Professional Reviews**: www.amazon.com
**Email**: LHarris@chpublishing.org

# Other Children's Heart Titles

*The Rise of Death Valley*
Loretta L. Harris
Illustrated by Ronald Thompson


*Who Did It and Why?*
Loretta L. Harris
Illustrated by Ronald Thompson

*Hard Life*
Loretta L. Harris
Illustrated by Ronald Thompson

*The Inside Struggle*
Loretta L. Harris
Illustrated by Ronald Thompson

*A Gangsta's Life*
Loretta L. Harris
Illustrated by Ronald Thompson

*Through the Eyes of a Poet*
Loretta L. Harris
Illustrated by Ellis Boaz

## Available at:

**Children's Heart Bookstore**
**Baker and Taylor**
**Amazon Bookstore**
**Barnes and Nobles**
**Books-A-Million**
**Borders Bookstore**

## Everywhere Books are Sold!

# Appendix A

## Hospital Pictures

*Chapter One: Green Honda Civic at Johnson's Wrecker*

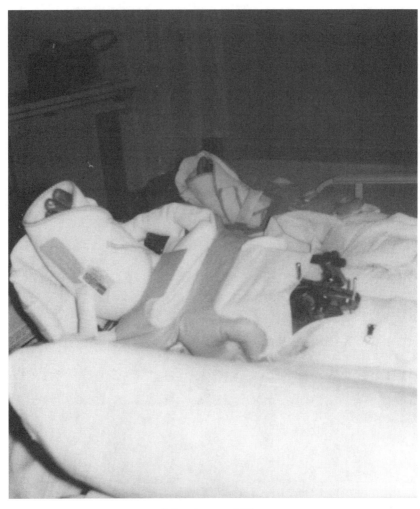

*Chapter Two: Left leg External Fixator*

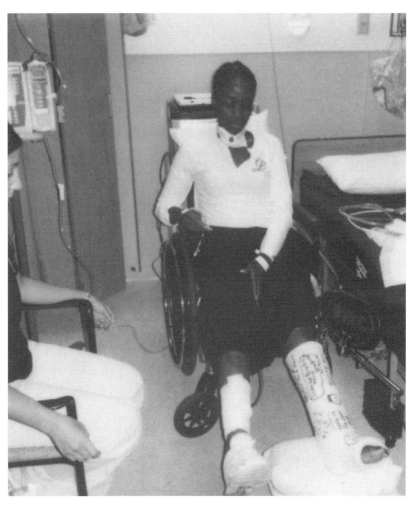

*Chapter Four Lucerne Hospital Room 420*

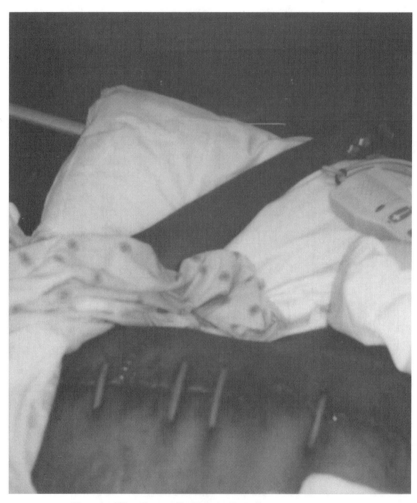

*Chapter Six: Stomach Suture Bands*

# Appendix B

## Seven Steps To Developing
## A Conqueror's Mentality

## Activity Journal

**Step 1:**
Face Your Adversity

**Step 2:**
Release Your Frustrations

**Step 3:**
Seek Counsel

**Step 4:**
Search the Scriptures

**Step 5:**
Develop Faith-Filled Confessions

**Step 6:**
Recognize Lessons Learned

**Step 7:**
Take a Stand

# Seven Steps To Developing A Conqueror's Mentality

## Activity Journal

## Step 1

**Task:** Describe your present adversity.

**Reference:** There will be an opportunity on your journey to recovery when you must come face to face with your tragedy (Chapter 3).

Date:_____

_____

_____

_____

_____

_____

_____

_____

_____

_____

_____

_____

_____

_____

_____

_____

_____

_____

_____

_____

_____

130

## Step 2

**Task:** Release your inner-thoughts and questions.

**Reference:** *We don't have a priest who is out of touch with our reality. He's been through weakness and testing, expe- rienced it all—all but the sin. So let's walk right up to him and get what he is so ready to give. Take the mercy, accept the help* (Hebrews 4:14-15).

## Step 3

**Task:** Schedule an interview with someone who has survived a similar tragedy.

**Reference:** *In every situation you face in life, just know that someone has been right where you are. Take notes and learn from that person* (Chapter 11).

**Interviewee:**

_____

**Date:**

_____

**Time:**

_____

**Discussion:**

_____

_____

_____

_____

_____

_____

_____

_____

_____

_____

_____

_____

## Step 4

**Task:** Research scriptures and inspirational quotes designed to encourage your victory.

**Reference:** *No weapon that is formed against me shall prosper* (Isaiah 54:17, KJV).

_____

_____

_____

_____

_____

_____

_____

_____

_____

_____

_____

_____

_____

_____

_____

_____

_____

_____

## Step 5

*Task:* Create daily confessions.

*Reference: If you have to start from ground zero before you can get back on your feet, do just that with a smile. I dedicated my mornings to constant medita-tion and recitation of faith-filled confessions* (Chapter 7).

_____

_____

_____

_____

_____

_____

_____

_____

_____

_____

_____

_____

_____

_____

_____

_____

_____

## Step 6

**Task:** Now that you have over-come adversity, explain the lessons learned.

**Reference:** *When you make a decision to take the journey less traveled, you triumph not only for yourself but also for that person whose life will be impacted by your story of survival.* (Chapter 11).

_____

_____

_____

_____

_____

_____

_____

_____

_____

_____

_____

_____

_____

_____

## Step 7

**Task**: Take a stand today! Explain how you will live the triumphant life!

**Reference**: *When faced with life altering circumstances, ask yourself this simple question, "What do I have to live for?"* (Chapter11).

_____

_____

_____

_____

_____

_____

_____

_____

_____

_____

_____

_____

_____

_____

_____

_____

_____

# Endnotes

## Chapter 1

Barr, V. (2008, May 19). The Day of the Accident.
(L. Harris, Interviewer)
Bonner, A. M. (2008, May 8). The Day of the Accident.
(L. Harris, Interviewer)
Harris, C. (2008, January 5). The Day of the Accident.
(L. Harris, Interviewer)
Harris, D. (2008, January 1). The Day of the Accident.
(L. Harris, Interviewer)
Harris, K. (2008, May 15). The Day of the Accident.
(L. Harris, Interviewer)
Harris, M. B. (2008, June 29). The Day of the Accident.
(L. Harris, Interviewer)
Harris, M. (2008, January 15). The Day of the Accident.
(L. Harris, Interviewer)
Ingram, C. (2008, June 2). The Day of the Accident.
(L. Harris, Interviewer)
Jackson, D. (2008, June 25). The Day of the Accident.
(L. Harris, Interviewer)
Jackson, M. (2008, June 25). The Day of the Accident.
(L. Harris, Interviewer)
Neal, M. (2008, May 14). The Day of the Accident.
(L. Harris, Interviewer)
Summers, T. (2008, June 2). The Day of the Accident.
(L. Harris, Interviewer)
Medical, W. T. (n.d.). Abdominal Compartment
Syndrome.org. Retrieved June 29, 2008, from
Overview: Intra-abdominal hypertension
and abdominal compartment syndrome:
http://www.abdominal-compartment-
syndrome.org/acs/overview.html

## Chapter 2

Block, E. F. (2008). Placement of postpyloric feeding tube.
Orlando: Orlando Regional Healthcare System.
Callahan, G. S. (2006). Subtotal gastrectomy.
Orlando: Orlando Regional Healthcare System.

Gupta, B. R. (2006). Complex repair of multiple facial lacerations and avulsion injuries. Orlando: Orlando Regional Healthcare System.

Munro, M. W. (2006). Irrigation and debridement: Primary closure of upper arm wound. Orlando: Orlando Regional Healthcare System.

Munro, M. W. (2006). Open reducation and internal fixation of left iliac wing fracture. Orlando: Orlando Regional Healthcare System.

Munro, M. W. (2008). Open reduction and internal fixation. Orlando: Orlando Regional Healthcare System.

Munro, M. W. (2006). Resuscitation of the patient in the operating room suite. Orlando: Orlando Regional Healthcare System.

Quijada, P. B. (2006). Closure of the abdomen. Orlando: Orlando Regional Healthcare System.

Reuter, N. (2006). Exploratory laparotomy. Orlando: Orlando Regional Healthcare System.

Smith, H. G. (2008). Placement of the Vac-pac. Orlando: Orlando Regional Healthcare System.

## Chapter 3

Kubler-Ross, E. (1969). On death and dying: What the dying have to teach doctors, nurses, clergy and their own families. New York: The Macmillan Company.

## Chapter 4

Harris, L. (2006). Goals. Orlando: Loretta Harris.

## Chapter 5

Harris, L. (2006). Lucerne rehab. Orlando: Loretta Harris.

Kubler-Ross, E. (1969). On death and dying: What the dying have to teach doctors, nurses, clergy and their own families. New York: Macmillan Co.

## Chapter 6

Jackson, M. (2008). The voice of the lord in the midst of the storm. Orlando: The River of Life Christian Center.

## Chapter 8

Haskins, J. (1977). The life and death of martin luther king, jr. New York: Beech Tree Books.
Jakoubek, R. (2005). Martin luther king, jr: Civil rights leader. Philadelphia: Chelsea House Publishers an imprint of Infobase Publishing.
Merriam-Webster Online Dictionary. (n.d.). Retrieved 2006, from www.merriam-webster.com

## Chapter 10

Harris, L. (2008). Overcoming Adversity. Orlando: Children's Heart Publishing.
Harris, L. (2006). Victim statement. Orlando: Loretta Harris.

## Chapter 11

Strong, J. (1990). The New Strong's Exhaustive Concordance of the Bible. Nashville: Thomas Nelson Publishers. Major Religions of the World Ranked by Number of Adherents. (n.d.). Retrieved June 30, 2008, from Adherents.com: http://www.adherents.com

## Chapter 12

Barr, V. (2008, May 19). Testimonial. (L. Harris, Interviewer)
Bonner, A. M. (2008, May 8). Testimonial.

(L. Harris, Interviewer)
Ford, M. (2008, May 24). Testimonial.
(L. Harris, Interviewer)
Ingram, C. (2008, June 2). Testimonial.
(L. Harris, Interviewer)
Jackson, A. (2008, May 23). Testimonial.
(L. Harris, Interviewer)
Jackson, A. (2008, June 2). Testimonial.
(L. Harris, Interviewer)
Neal, M. (2008, May 14). Testimonial.
(L. Harris, Interviewer)
Stewart, S. (2008, May 20). Testimonial.
(L. Harris, Interviewer)
Summers, T. (2008, June 2). Testimonial.
(L. Harris, Interviewer)